Letters from

ERASTUS

Field Notes
on Grace

ANNE D. EMERSON

Levellers Press, Amherst, Massachusetts
Printed in the United States of America
ISBN 978-1-937146-70-2

To my grandchildren,
Eamon and Margaret

Table of Contents

Prologue

This is a book about people we have lost, the living and the dead, and the unexpected ways they return to us. History, after all, is forever repeating itself, especially in families.

The names of the immediate family of Lincoln have been changed to protect their privacy. In all other instances real names are used.

I

Sorrow sits at breakfast
holding hands with me...

JANUARY, 2010. LINCOLN WAS SENT TO BRIDGEWATER last month, his latest, maybe his last, stop in the Massachusetts criminal justice system. The prison for the "criminally insane." Funny phrase that. As though it were criminal to be insane. He is my cousin Ruthie's son. My daughter Hannah's childhood playmate. We call him Linc. He strangled a man he thought was molesting his child. That was seven years ago.

This morning I am sitting at the breakfast table with my daughter Hannah reading my pile of newspapers. We live in Jamaica Plain, Massachusetts. Peter and I bought our big house with my two little daughters back in the early eighties, long before we were married. In those days there were few buyers for houses in JP. White families with children had fled this neighborhood in the seventies when school busing was mandated, and we were in the first trickle back. It is more than twenty-five years since we moved here and this kitchen has seen a lot.

Hannah and I are eating breakfast in a bright stream of winter light with the birds murmuring contentedly at the feeder outside the window. The *Herald* is open to a headline that reads "Defendant attacks Hub Defense Lawyer." I read it out loud to her. It describes a courtroom brawl in which Linc lunges at his attorney after accusing him of poisoning his cranberry juice and his assistant of running over his dog. All this at the beginning of a trial for assaulting a correctional officer at Bridgewater State Hospital.

At this point he is not even close to serving his real time, a manslaughter sentence that will eventually be done in North Carolina if they ever finish with him in Massachusetts.

I read it to Hannah and she makes a little laugh, a choked sound, as if she's holding the sadness high in her throat, away from her heart.

"What dog?" she asks.

Linc has achieved some modest notoriety as a dangerous inmate. In his own mind he is a vigilante, carefully selecting scum for his outrage. Not too long ago he attacked Neil Entwistle, the Brit convicted of murdering his wife and baby and fleeing the country. Finding a way to be on the heroic side seems to enable his violence.

I feel very weary reading this. I hope that my cousin Ruthie is numb by now and cannot feel this pain any more. Someone once said you are only as happy as your least happy child, and if that is true, having a child in prison must be like a permanent purgatory.

Later that day I find the article on the internet, with 31 comments. I start to read them. From Raven 1 we have: *How much money does it cost to house all these murderers, and how much do the lawyers reap with the endless appeals, all tax money? Bring back the death penalty. If there is no doubt someone is guilty of murder put them to death in a timely fashion. The majority of people in this state are FOR the death penalty. It is the democrats on Beacon Hill stifling the will of the people. Vote out all democrats!*

From another commentator, Rick b637: *who cares hes a smug scumy lawyer and hell that other guy did put a beating on that baby killer entwistle so two thumbs up to that.*

I stop there. It feels like there is a hot coil in the pit of my stomach. This troubled cousin of mine is in the public domain now, like an old mad dog for people to kick around. People who cannot even spell; people who feel entitled to spew hate. They don't know this man. Maybe the *Herald* should have picked up the story that he ran a marathon inside his cell last year. One hundred and seven laps across constituted a mile, he figured, so on April

17, Patriots Day, he ran for four straight hours. That would be a pretty good story. Not that Linc gets to read any of these papers, much less see the blogs. He would probably be quite proud if he saw all the news coverage he's getting. But not the blogs. He wouldn't like those. Their cacophony is just like the voices in his head.

In my mind I have a picture of Linc as a little boy with a big head of tussled brown hair and a very tattered blanket, trailing after his sisters to our family chapel in Maine. Of his dragon slaying costume and his wooden sword. Working in tandem with Hannah on the beach splitting rocks in an impassioned search for stalactites. They were the youngest in a cohort of five, Linc the single boy.

The family chapel was built on a high granite ledge in the forest of Dog Island Point by Linc's grandfather, my uncle, in 1931 on land shared by our large extended family that my grandfather and his two close friends had purchased in 1914. Warm summer afternoons linger in the sanctuary like fairy dust, leaving the smells of old baking timbers, burnt candles and cedar branches. I never go into the chapel without feeling the intense presence of my ancestors, like ice and fire in my heart. We sing their hymns and perform their rituals. I feel their awe, their sadness, their gratitude, as if I had swallowed them whole.

Linc and I have gone to that chapel and sung "Eternal Father Strong to Save" and "America the Beautiful" for most of the summers of our lives. He may not remember some of those ancestors, but they are in him nonetheless. Maybe even in some of the voices he hears. I am sure he dreams of the tall pines and hears the chapel bell even in his prison cell, and he is luckier than most to have them to summon.

The matriarch of the family was Grandma Josephine. She would be appalled to know that her great grandson, who bears her proud maiden name in the middle of his, has achieved such notoriety in the *Boston Herald*. I loved my grandma, but she scared me too. I can almost hear her arch New England voice calling my own mother "The Beauty" in that kind of capital B way that made her seem very far off, which I think Grandma wished she were. My mother was an outsider in this old New England group, a larky woman from small town Canada with legendary eyes. She died when I was five and I was told she had gone to heaven. How could she have left me behind?

You would think that the memories would dim with time, but this one bone hard fact is like a missing rib. It left a cavity in me, a cold empty space that can fill suddenly with surprisingly unpleasant things, like a dense wet fog. When she died I was just on the edge of memory, the dream state of narrative. Bogeyman territory.

A piece of your soul goes on walkabout when you lose a parent early in life; trying to coax it home can be a lifelong enterprise. Among the acknowledged long-term effects of the death of a parent on a child is a twofold increase in the prospects of depression. But I have never heard anyone talk about the effects of losing one of the most important listeners in your life, a sounding board for your growing up. And if you lose your listener, you may lose your voice. The sensation is like becoming invisible.

Maybe the other parent can pick up the slack or maybe, like my father, they are curled up in their own grief. Dad was a doctor, a scientist, and a New Englander trained to keep his emotions in check. He tried to distract my brother and me from ours. He spent long hours in his laboratory at the hospital and we saw less and less of him and more and more of our grandmothers. He took us to the Episcopal Church, in which he found a familiar comfort and I, the torture of having to sit still. Once when I was nine, I put my hymnal down on the long shelf in front of my pew and the entire thing came crashing down in the middle of the Benediction, an occasion so mortifying that I can still feel the hot flush that came over me, like the brand of the Devil.

I spend some part of every summer in East Penobscot Bay with various cousins, some seventy of us in total. I am closest to Ruthie, Linc's mother. She has exuberant auburn hair, even now, and a deep, low laugh. We had our children in the same seasons, and our daughters are best friends for life. The older girls played "church" together, taking turns giving communion and muttering benedictions.

We all swim together in the same stream of ancestors and feed like guppies on their legacies to us, known and unknown. The constellation of this family is well documented. They save things, like sailing trophies—and letters. They have a genealogy. But they are very tight-lipped about it all. Very private. They would not like to be blogged about.

December, 2001. Let us go back a few years and begin this story at Christmastime, the Christmas that followed the fall of the Twin Towers, when I was reading Emily Dickinson's biography and George Bush was bombing Afghanistan. Linc was muddling through somewhere, selling newspapers, and not particularly on my radar screen. I was alone in our big house, feeling very down. Peter was in Kansas City for a seven-year contract with the KC Repertory Theater and my grown children were off in their own lives. I was leading a project to develop a history museum in Boston and I couldn't leave, so we had bought a little bungalow in Kansas City for Peter and picked out a minimalist collection of furnishings from our JP house to send out to the Midwest. We had agreed we would not worry about the commuting costs; we would just fly back and forth every other weekend. I was fifty-four and this would be the first time in my life I had ever lived alone. I had gone from my childhood home to a college dorm to marriage, babies, and a second marriage with hardly an overnight on my own. I had been cooking for a husband and a family for thirty-one years, day in and day out; working full time all but two of those years. When your life is full you are propelled through it, and you have no time to contemplate the absent listener.

Since Peter had started in Kansas City I had been in a state of mind that I can best describe as agitated blankness. I was filling my life to the brim, working twelve hours a day, scheduling every minute with something, but there wasn't a gram of pleasure in any of it. There was not even anyone to cook for. I was emptied out, like a beach at low tide. When I look at what happened next I think that maybe that blankness made for a kind of receptivity.

I went one day to a conference at the Massachusetts Historical Society. The museum I was working on would focus much of its attention on the untold stories of the Boston region, those of African Americans and Irish, Asian and other immigrant communities. The conference that day was on African-American history in Boston.

The Massachusetts Historical Society is an imposing place with a locked, filigreed steel-over-glass front door symbolic of an old New England privacy. It is like a mine with millions of glittering veins, some of them mica, some of them gold. Its vast archives sit largely untouched year after year, while researchers turn over the same nuggets of Adamses, Emersons, Longfellows and Alcotts, looking for new clues to the old greats. As I ring the bell that morning for admittance to the conference I think about our friend August Wilson whose cycle of plays on the black experience Peter has produced over the past years. My most intimate encounters with black culture have been through the living rooms and back porches of August's plays, ten of them in all, one for each decade of the twentieth century. His ancestors lived inside of him and he could spin out their stories and hear their voices telling them. A shimmering presence in many of them is Aunt Esther, born at the dawn of slavery in America and now a character in August's plays who lives in the hill district of Pittsburgh, disseminating wisdom at three-hundred-something years old. These plays had planted in my mind the idea that had driven my museum interest: that a tiny fragment of a story, or a simple object like the shackles of a fugitive slave in a museum case, could bring a sharp burst of empathy and understanding to an otherwise blank and indifferent heart.

August would have found this imposing venue for a conference on African American history very ironic: blacks would probably have been sent to the delivery entrance until well into the twentieth century. Whatever physical evidence of their lives and histories might survive, it is not within these walls. There are, however, boxes and boxes of my family papers in here. I have never in my more than fifty years looked at them and have no real idea what might be in them, so I am planning to spend my lunch break doing a little investigating.

The computerized finding-aid describes the entire collection. Twenty-three boxes in all. They are a jumble of my father's ancestors, Sewalls, Emersons, Hopkinses. The first three boxes contain odds and ends: a seventeenth century receipt from Samuel Sewall, a few letters from my grandmother's parents and siblings. My grandmother was a Sewall, my grandfather Kendall Emerson's mother was Mary Annette Hopkins. The computer lists boxes and boxes of correspondence between Mary Annette Hopkins Emerson and her mother, Charlotte Freylinghuysen Allen Hopkins. Fifty years of back and forth from Amherst to Northampton, a distance of nine miles. I fill out the order form for box four where their correspondence begins and hand it to the librarian. Waiting for her return, I absently stare at the afternoon sunlight shimmering on the bookshelves. I am suspended between centuries like those little motes of dust caught in the shaft of light.

Within minutes the librarian is back carrying a grey box that she deposits with meticulous care on my table in the reading room. She turns on the green shaded lamp, hands me a magnifying glass and gives me a few hushed instructions. Box four contains a series of acid-free folders, each dated, with a small collection of letters inside. Letters on white paper, embossed with a small seal. Letters on blue paper in a spidery back slanting hand. And little ink smudged notes in childish hand.

*Dear Nettie, How de do? Grandmas at our house I am at school
when I was coming I saw the cunningest little thing ever first I
saw some soldiers then I saw some firemen pulling a fire engine
and then came a man driving it and then on the wagon there
was TOM THUM'S CARRIAGE the sweetest little thing you
ever saw the horses were not so big as your rocking horse. I want
to say more but there is not room. Mallie*

My grandfather, Kendall had a sister named Malleville. This
one must have been a generation earlier. Such a strange big name
for this little hand to carry.

A folded piece of stationery with a stamp saying, "Merchant's
Line Bain's Telegraph Office, 76 State Street, Boston, April 3,
1852," turns out to be a letter from Erastus Hopkins to his daughter Nettie on her fourth birthday.

*I see Swinton, Caro, Lottie, and Johnny all sitting in Mama's
lap with Annie close alongside. See if you can't cuddle up close
and make room for her too. Try now. Snuggle up.*

*My heart aches, there are so many little folks in it. I wonder if
I can take care of them all. Tell mama I wish I could be one of her
babies and feel the comfort which you feel when you hug her up so
nicely. Kiss Mama and the whole lap full for me. Your dear father.*

And then a penciled note in a child's hand from New York,
May 23, 1856:

*Dear Nettie, I am so sorry that dear little Johnnie is dead and
that you have been so sick and I hope that Lottie will get well.
Where did they bury little Johnny? In the graveyard or the
garden? I think that he has gone to heaven and that he would be
a great deal happier than he ever was. I hope that we shall all be
good and go there too. Your affectionate cousin, Willie Smith*

I feel myself dropping into a rabbit hole, a small fist pressing
into my chest. Each little note calls up an intimate lost world. I

am almost suffocated by a wave of longing to know these people, to see and touch the landmarks of their lives. Since I was a little girl I have had a simple bow-fronted bureau that has traveled with me wherever I've moved. Stuck inside the top drawer, on a red bordered sticker in my grandma's handwriting is the name Annette Hopkins. I had never really given much thought to who Annette Hopkins was. Now I am staring at the baby notes written by her father and cousin to Little Nettie, who would become my great grandmother. Was this her little brother, Johnnie, who died? I know nothing of this branch of my family. If I hadn't had this hour of pause in this bruising month of sadness, I might never have known they lived.

Suddenly my reverie is broken. The librarian is chastising the woman across from me for picking up something in her file. "Please leave the contents of your folder flat," she commands. I am reluctantly back in my body, which is radiating resistance to this officious person. She has not yet spied me turning these letters in every direction to decipher the handwriting. These are my ancestors, and until a few years ago these papers had been held for a hundred years, some for two hundred years, by members of my family in their homes. I want to take them back.

But then I have to admire how they have been organized and carefully filed in chronological order and placed in acid free boxes. If they were at my house I might have piled them in the attic or a damp basement and forgotten them. I might never have read them. Here they have been consecrated, made holy.

Reluctantly, I close the folder, slide it carefully back into Box Four and return to the conference. All afternoon I have that feeling you get when you've just met someone you really want to get to know and you're contemplating your next move. These people aren't going anywhere, but my life is a jumble of work and managing a commuting marriage. The Library isn't open in the evening or on weekends. How am I ever going to know what's in these twenty-three boxes of almost illegible handwriting?

II

*A little message freighted
with an untold weight of love*

I MANAGE A RETURN VISIT TO THE LIBRARY only because they decide to extend their hours one evening a week. This time I ask for Box Five, even though I haven't finished Box Four. I have an urgent need to figure out who is living in these boxes. It feels like an almost insurmountable task. The handwriting makes my jaw ache. By Box Five Nettie is twelve, her handwriting full of ink blots and emotion. I can almost see her hormones surging on the page in the big round swirls that shift from a forward to a backward slant. Her mother, Charlotte, has tiny spidery writing, done with the finest point pen, a torture to read. All the m's are upside down and the letter I, a giant ampersand. Nettie's father, Erastus, has the steadiest hand, but always with little patches faint upon the page. Then I come to two letters that I have no trouble at all reading. The Library is almost entirely dark, but for my little green shaded lamp. I plummet back down the rabbit hole, into another century, another spiritual realm.

Northampton, June 1, 1862

My Dear Caro,

*I bear you on my heart daily. We love to hear from you
and of you and of your studious habits and program. This
information, however, comes almost entirely from yourself; yet
we trust the verity of your reports. And now I send this little
winged message which, though small, goes freighted with an*

untold weight of love. Be good, my darling and deserve it all and vastly more. Somehow, I am, and have always been in the habit of expecting great things of you; not by dashes, but by passionate and all conquering fidelity. It is June, the face of nature is in its loveliness. No wonder that I love you, for this is your natal month, the most fitting month of the twelve for lovely and beautiful ladies to be born in and catch the temper of the skies. Roses were round your cradle-they adorned your pale mother's hair, as she lay upon her bed with her sweet, insubstantial bud nestling in her life-giving bosom. That bosom was the sweetest, safest place you were ever in, and will always be the sweetest and the safest until you pass to the bosom of your Heavenly Father.

 Your loving father, Erastus Hopkins

And then this letter, written, I realized much later, when Nettie had just battled a potentially fatal childhood disease.

       Northampton, December 14, 1862

 My Dear Annette,

  ...Set your heart upon heavenly things. Then (you) will be always young ... as the day & hour approaches when you are to enter upon a life of joy which will never fade away. Put your little heart there now. Call Christ to you and deposit the treasure in the palm of his outstretched hand and call on him daily to lead you like a lamb to do his will; to be always gentle, pure, full of love, self denial, to be delighted in the prosecution and attainment of knowledge and true wisdom. And when you think that in a thought or feeling you have departed from the gentleness or purity of his sweet example, go and confess it and seek remedy in his strength and blessing.

  I want, my dear Nettie, to be his, more than I want you to be mine.

 Your dear father, Erastus Hopkins

Northampton Dec 14ᵃ 1862

My dear Annette,

We keep thinking of you all the time. If you should ever, in coming years, be situated as I am, you will know with what tender love, & anxiety a parent thinks of an absent suffering child. How God teaches you of his goodness, granting to you the presence & constant attentions of a mother who loves you more than she loves herself, & who is to you what no one else can be. Before she was as old as you, she had no such mother to love & care for her. Sickness & sickness would have been to her very different from what they now are to you.

We are led to hope, from mama's letter of Friday, that you are getting better, but we still feel anxious, & shall continue to feel so until we have further assurance.

If, as we hope, you are truly convalescent, then you will have time, on your bed, & in your sick chamber to think of what you have passed through again & again & even again, you are admonished to cherish & constantly utter the prayer so beautifully expressed in these words,

"Be this my one great business here,
With holy trembling, holy fear,
To make my calling sure!
Thine utmost counsel to fulfill,
And suffer all thy righteous will,
And to the end endure!"

It was as if this man had written directly to me, bypassing all these intervening generations. "Put your little heart there now. Call Christ to you and deposit the treasure in his outstretched hand and call on him daily to lead you like a lamb to do his will...." Why had I never heard mention of this great grandfather with his sweet commanding voice? How had all this emotional eloquence dissipated through the generations? Who was Erastus, this man so full of love and faith and beautiful prose?

Interspersed among the Hopkins family letters were letters from my great grandfather's parents, Emersons who lived in Nashua, New Hampshire. The contrast gave me a hint as to why these poetic, spiritual letters had gone unnoticed. There surely could be no less imaginative or poetic people than these hardworking, thrifty Emersons, no matter that they were second cousins to Ralph Waldo and living in his time and neighborhood. Their letters were full of monetary and health worries, of train schedules, and subtle chastisement. This is the branch that passed on the concentrated elixir of shame, that Puritan antidote to all things joyful that leads to the deep desire to be invisible and disconnected. I know the type in my own family, and encounter it all too frequently in the dark and anxious part of myself.

I pick up a stubby number two pencil and copy these two letters word for word. It would be years before I would have the time to delve deeply into this voluminous material; but for now I will hold these letters close. They are addressed to me just as surely as they are addressed to Nettie and Caroline. Each time I read them I feel a current of love surge through me.

If my mother had written her heart to my brother and me as she lay dying would those letters have whispered us through the hard times ahead? We have such tiny fragments to conjure her with. A suitcase, a few photos, a silver compact. Her memory seems more petrified in them than living. But conjuring her is a lifetime pursuit for both of us, no matter how scant the materials.

I copied Erastus's words on a bright piece of paper and put them up on the refrigerator. I quoted them in letters of condo-

lence to friends in distress, telling them that I had discovered
them in the letters of an ancestor, which somehow made it seem
ok, more neutral, not as if I were pushing religion on them. I
could read these words and in an instant be lifted above whatever
petty daily struggle I was in. Erastus was leading me like a lamb.

Who was this Erastus? There was very little more about him
in the MHS Library. I found a biographical snippet that told me
he was a preacher born in 1810 in Hadley, Massachusetts, and a
daguerreotype, described in the catalogue as the "Founders of
the Free Soil Party, 1852." When the librarian brought it to me,
I looked at the five men and I wanted him to be the one in the
middle, almost the way you would if you were adopting a child
and you weren't sure which one was yours. I got my wish. He is
strikingly handsome, with his face turned in partial profile to the
camera. His eyebrows slant down at the corners and his light hair
and beard suggest that his eyes were blue. You had to sit stock still
for a daguerreotype so everyone looks like they're striking a pose.
But his is the magnetic face in the group and his central position
suggests that he was their leader. He would have been forty-two.

When I saw the picture I was flooded with relief. It matched
the majestic voice. My love was, so far, untarnished.

Erastus Hopkins, center, and co-founders of the Free Soil Party in Massachusetts. (Photo courtesy of Massachusetts Historical Society.)

III

I Bear You on My Heart Daily

I PAUSE COMING OUT OF A DOCTOR'S OFFICE one day to squirt some hand sanitizer into my palms and suddenly I am five years old holding on to a pink rubber doll. The smell has flooded me with love for this beloved toy, as though it were in my arms right now. We all are packed with memories, tucked away like the ping-pong balls and old fuses in my kitchen junk drawer, waiting to be called into service. When I mourn the passing of a relative, Peter says, "If the relationship was so important, why didn't you spend more time with him?" Because, I answer, these are the memories I carry, that are part of me and make me who I am. They don't need to be updated all the time.

We can pick and choose from all the twists and turns in our lives and construct our own narrative, but some memories are deeply locked in, and arrive unbidden in living technicolor whether we want them or not.

Other memories are like scaffolding, turning points in the whole narrative, like the day Linc went to prison in the spring of 2003.

Peter and I were together with our daughters, Jody and Hannah, in Kansas City when we heard the news, and the moment is indelibly imprinted on our minds because just minutes before we had driven through a tornado. The storm had come upon us halfway through the twenty-mile trip back to the airport. The blue sky turned in a moment to smoky carbon black and the car began shaking like a tin can in a disposal, hammered by huge hailstones. We could see the inky columns swirling in the distance. Panicked drivers were packing their cars under the overpasses, or abandoning them by the road and running to shelter under their concrete arches. I was gripped by the image of all of us being sucked into a black funnel, like a meat grinder, and flung out into the stratosphere.

We were each in character, acting out our terror. I was the mother of steel, clamped to the wheel, willing myself to see through the shuddering black wall of water. Peter, in the front passenger seat, his voice icy calm, constructed his own reality of minimal danger as the radio screeched its emergency alerts, warning of three tornados converging on the airport. Hannah, our twenty-something youngest, was in take-charge mode, alternately begging and ordering me to pull over so we could get out and hide under an overpass. Her older sister Jody was screaming at her to shut up.

Wracking my brain for something additional to do to save us, I began to mutter a prayer. It was right out of that letter Erastus had written to Nettie.

"Here I am Lord, in awe of your power, my heart, my family all in the palm of your hand. We are your lambs. Lead us Lord through this darkness...." I muttered variations on this theme for some minutes under my breath. Then, almost as suddenly as the darkness had descended the rain abated, the sun came out and we got to the airport just as the people who had been evacuated into the underground garage were being let out.

We sat down, dazed and anxious, at a café table and Jody's phone rang. As she listened we watched her body curl like a leaf drying up. Her hand went slowly up to her mouth and a layer of tears welled in her huge blue eyes. When she hung up she said "That was Grace. Lincoln strangled Jane's boyfriend. He's been arrested."

My mind was a mire of tangled thoughts. My own family brought to safety and my dear cousin's smashed with grief. We sat in stunned silence. Linc: Mark and Ruthie's beloved son. Hannah's playmate, born in the same summer. That would make him twenty-nine. He had been a troubled kid since his adolescence, but it was the kind of trouble adolescents get into: sex, drugs and petty thievery. They had sent him to a special school and all his family worked to support him in a twelve-step program. He had run away with a classmate, Jane, a strange and angry girl whom I had met just once. Not many people scare me, but she did. They had a son. They were married. And divorced.

He had taken the bus from Boston to North Carolina fueled by fury. Something Jane had said made him decide that her boyfriend was molesting one of the children in the house. His son Noah lived there with his two step siblings. Linc was a champion wrestler in high school and a headlock can be a deadly weapon. Now he is in the county jail in Raleigh, North Carolina and Mark has flown down. Ruthie is alone grieving with her daughters. I call her when I get home and she repeats in a monotone the story we have just heard. It will be a long time before we'll hear her beautiful laugh again.

When I get back to Boston I go to church for the first time in years. It is a black church, about a mile from my house and I go because I want to hear my friend Ray Hammond preach. I had travelled with him on a work-related expedition to San Francisco, sat with his family at the famous black gospel church, Glide Memorial. I want to see him in action.

I feel distinctly like a tourist in this church, or an invisible audience member at one of August Wilson's plays. I come to Bethel African Methodist Episcopal Church on time and fidget, almost alone, in the gymnasium where the service is to be held. Gradually it fills with drumming and singing and dancing. I recognize a surprising number of people from my work in the city including a few white people who I know are loyal to this church. For an hour the praise singing goes on, led by four jazz musicians and a choir. The rhythms have a hypnotic effect that gradually let me put away my self-consciousness and distracting thoughts. Then Ray Hammond comes out, and it occurs to me suddenly that his name is not Raymond, but Ray, and for good reason. His effect on this crowd is just like a shaft of sunlight. He invites visitors to stand and say their names, and where they come from. Then he looks out and sees me. He smiles his great smile and introduces me to the congregation. So much for being invisible.

He preaches a sermon meticulously woven around a biblical text taken from Prophets. It will stay with me as the three P sermon: prophesy, prayer and persistence. He introduces each theme like the elements of a fugue, weaving in humor and anecdote, and building from a whisper to a great crescendo, as if his voice is a full orchestra. It feels like he has created this sermon just for me; I connect to every element. Prophesy he defines as speaking the truth, an idea so simple and graspable, that it gives me an entirely new outlook on the Bible.

Ray's sermon goes on for an astonishing forty-five minutes and has every person sitting on these hard folding chairs listening closely. Some shout out "preach, pastor, preach!" when they are most moved.

He ends with a "call to prayer," inviting us to the altar if we choose, or to pray with a neighbor. My Episcopalian blood runs cold with dread. The essence of our service is anonymity. I have not a clue how to pray beyond the rote recitations of the Book of Common Prayer and my few lines from Erastus. But here comes Cheryl. Out of the corner of my eye I see a large black woman with bright yellow hair and a great light in her eyes making a beeline for me. She offers me her hands and asks if I would like to pray. There is no getting out of this; I look around and see the congregation splitting off into pairs and small groups, bending their heads together in the fluorescent glare of the gymnasium lights. Our two blond heads, bowed together, must stand out in this sea of black.

I take a deep breath and murmur, "OK."

"What would you like to pray about?" she asks. I rack my brain for a topic.

"I'd like to pray for our community." I am instantly embarrassed by my proposed topic. But she begins to pray like a sprinter and does not draw a breath for seven minutes. For seven minutes she washes me with the poetry of her visionary thoughts about what our community might be, with what sadnesses it is wracked, what hope and tragedy walk in our streets. She prays for the children coming home after school, for the gang members who have no hope of a future, for the politicians and the priests and for the elderly too fearful to leave their homes. She blesses me with the power of her exquisite outpouring. I have to learn to do this prayer thing. Out loud.

By the time the service is over, I know for sure what people mean by the Holy Spirit. It is palpable in this place. The next week I come twenty minutes late and am right on time. And before long I'm even dancing with my arms in the air and praying outloud, for Linc.

Time goes a long way to healing wounds. Over the years I see Mark and Ruthie every summer in Maine. Linc's incarceration is a fact of their lives but their lives have many other parts. They are raising Linc's son, Noah, a beautiful child with a musical gift. They have seven grandchildren, devoted daughters and lots of friends. Seven years after that tornado, in the spring of 2010, I find myself spending a week with them in Florida.

Linc is in the Middlesex County Jail. He has been shuffled between Bridgewater State Prison Hospital and Middlesex six times this year alone. Each time Bridgewater says he's not mentally ill, he's a sociopath and belongs in prison, not a mental hospital. His parents know differently. Bridgewater's director is a political appointment. There have been suicides and violent incidents at Bridgewater and this is bad for a political appointee. Send the dangerous ones back to the regular prison system. Mark and Ruthie would much rather have him in Bridgewater, bleak as it is. In the general prison population medicated prisoners are targets and that makes them reluctant to take their meds. Linc's parents are wondering if they will have to sue the state to get him proper care.

In our week together in Florida, Linc is like a ghost moving in and out of our thoughts. I want to talk about him; is it like inviting a black cloud into the room? But we do talk, and I can feel their relief that someone is willing to bring up the subject. One afternoon Mark and I are in a boat on the inland waterway, fishing. The motion comes back to me effortlessly: the curl of the finger to uncock the bale and hook the filament, the flick of the wrist. Then the line, looping out into the sky, catching on the wind, suspended for an instant as the lure drops to the water.

It's Thursday. On Tuesday of this week I had been at my Uncle Bill's funeral. Travelling seven hundred miles to my mother's old hometown in Ontario, I was the last one to arrive. He lay there, hands crossed, with that pouty mouth of his, as if he were waiting just for me. His maroon Shriner's hat, its tassle still, sat beside him, and someone had hung a fishing lure inside the casket. He was the one who taught me how to fish before memory began. Just that motion, that little flick, that arc fluttering to a cavern of shadow in the shivering misty dawn. "That's where the fish are, Annie," he whispered.

Mark and I cast silently, over and over into the sunset. I think of him teaching Linc this flick of the wrist and wonder if Linc remembers the moment he learned, or if it is just in that vast store of mute knowledge that flows from father to son.

IV

My dear dear Love: Sarah Bennett

PETER RETIRED FROM THE KANSAS CITY Repertory Theater in 2007. In all he had produced 150 plays in Missouri and at the Huntington in Boston since the early eighties, substantial, wonderful plays, that had been seen by over a million people. He came home and settled into a routine of listening systematically to his own extraordinary collection of jazz and classical music, and reading in his own assiduously collected library. I was envious as I left him at the breakfast table each morning and before long I was looking for a way to join him. I had been working full time in universities and not-for-profits for almost forty years. Every decade had been its own adventure: international population work; launching Boston's first successful not-for profit theater; administering a major international research center at Harvard; and finally developing the vision, and doing the political and fundraising work for a new history museum for Boston. For the last decade I had been in a frontline political job, always in the public eye, no way to be invisible. The work was far from completed but other champions had emerged. There were still many other things I wanted to do in my life. Being a frugal Yankee, I had saved for this moment. So I worked things out with my Board and joined Peter at the breakfast table.

The first thing I wanted to do with my newfound free time was go look for Erastus. The basic outlines of his life were not hard to find. He was born in Hadley, Massachusetts on April 7, 1810. He died in 1872. In his life he married, was widowed, married again, and in all, had nine children. He started out as a Presbyterian minister in South Carolina and within a decade had given it up. He became a Massachusetts State Legislator, President of the Connecticut River Railroad and a founder of the Free Soil Party. He had an older brother, Samuel who led the way into the ministry through the school hierarchy that Erastus followed: Boston Latin, Phillips Andover Academy, Dartmouth College, the Andover Theological School and Princeton Theological Seminary where he graduated in 1834. His sister married John Wheeler, the president of the University of Vermont. Erastus spent most of his life in Northampton, Massachusetts and was a leading citizen of the town in which he had grown up. His great grandmother was Esther Edwards, sister of the Northampton Calvinist preacher in the first "Great Awakening," Jonathan Edwards.

There's a big chunk of this puzzle of Erastus's life that doesn't quite fit, and it is captured by a little news clip from *The Liberator*, William Lloyd Garrison's radical abolitionist paper in Boston. The writer names Erastus specifically in a complaint in 1836: "a number of Presbyterian ministers…have moved south…some even marrying into slaveholding families." What's he doing in the plantation south? How odd it seems for this very New England young man from a well-known anti-slavery family to be the designated spiritual leader of a bunch of rice plantation owners in the South. His wife's name is Sarah Bennett. Who is this siren?

The South Carolina Historical Society has thirty letters that relate to Erastus, but they are too faded, they say, to copy for me. If I want to see them I have to go there myself. This is not exactly in my budget, but I will make it work. I book a flight to Charleston. The woman in line behind me in the jetway makes three bad jokes that seem loudly directed at me, about "damn Yankees, I mean damn Yankees, she says." She is not referring to the baseball team. What kind of South did Erastus move to? When did they start calling us damn Yankees? Not, I will find out, before the Civil

War; Charleston and Boston were intimately intertwined in the first part of the nineteenth century.

By placing an ad on Craig's List, I have found a room in Charleston in a beautiful private home that once did some time as a brothel. In the usual way that God or serendipity acts in our lives, the house is two doors down from Sarah and Erastus's brother-in-law's trading house at 12 State Street.

The letters that will provide my clues to Charleston in the 1830s are almost indecipherable. Many are cross-hatched, written first horizontally and then vertically, to save paper. Only the precision of the handwriting keeps me going. The first I read are from Sarah's devoted uncle, Thomas Napier, a Scotsman of the most sanctimonious stripe. He is playing Cupid, the secret go-between and advisor in the romance between Erastus and Sarah—whose parents are not keen on her marrying a minister. This is like reading a soap opera. Napier, like many Charlestonians, summered for years in Northampton. Sarah and her family often stayed with him and on one of these visits she met the handsome young Erastus. Napier was a bright social light in Northampton for many years, until it was discovered that his business in Charleston was slave trading. I wonder how Erastus took this when he found out.

Around the corner from my house in Charleston is the Slave Market Museum. This whole district was rife with slave trading right up through the Civil War. The importation of slaves was banned in 1808, but domestic slaves were a lucrative commodity, and they were thought of as just that: a commodity that was auctioned like porcelain from China or furniture from England. Sarah's sister Jane married Thomas Gadsden, a bank president who also traded in slaves in the building right down the street from where I am sleeping. In the block behind me is the warehouse of Thomas Napier. Today it is part of the Vendue Inn which boasts on its web site of the historic connection to Napier. In Charleston he was, and apparently still is, very well thought of.

Erastus went to South Carolina right out of Princeton Theological Seminary. He was vastly more mature than any twenty-four year old I know today, but he was also in love, just like you're supposed to be when you're twenty-four. Your biology is in charge. A shadow of Linc passes over me as I think of this stage of life. Linc who for so long has seemed to be a sixteen-year-old personality wrestling with his nearly middle aged body and out-of-control mind. Erastus was a man supremely in control, but it is at this moment in his life that I can see him struggling with his very passionate nature. In the one picture I have of him from this era he is slender and blond. Maybe a reddish blond. In the picture he looks solemn; he was a minister after all. But I imagine him in this southern place trying to fit in to please his wife, but standing out nonetheless, a little stiff and uneasy in this world of slaves and masters. He has arresting blue eyes that hold another's gaze without looking away. He is not impulsive, but he makes judgments. He thinks things through carefully and when he makes friends he is fiercely loyal, but watch out for his wrath.

After their wedding Erastus went off to Beech Island, some two hundred miles away from Charleston, where he would be appointed the Presbyterian Minister. It was a tough, backwoods environment and Sarah would stay in Charleston, living with her sister. She would soon give birth to their son, William Swinton Bennett Hopkins, named for her father.

On June 4, 1836 Erastus writes from Beech Island:

This day, my dear, dear, love, is our preparatory lecture & the communion is to be administered. I have seated myself with these objects before me, but …I will converse with you a moment as I would if you were here. Do you remember how you used to have your daily seat in my lap & what comfort we used to have? It is now more than three long months since we have enjoyed those seasons. I confess that I never felt so before, & do hope that we shall never be so separated again. I, in some measure, anticipated

all this trial when you concluded to go to Charleston. I knew
that it would be *a peculiar trial to me* to be here and have you be
there, but the reality has vastly surpassed all I anticipated.

My dearest, I do love you. Can you doubt it? And can you
be happy in my love? I have been thinking of our little boy &
have just selected a text and commenced upon a sermon to be
preached on the day he is to be baptized. I hope it will be a good
sermon. I doubt not it will be a feeling one. …As for Swinton,
I never write his name or speak of him, without feeling that I
do not <u>know</u> him, & then this begets a feeling so <u>painful</u>—that
it makes it painful for me to think of him. I <u>shall</u> have pleasure
in him, but hitherto he has caused me more pain than pleasure.
Then I cannot bear to have such feelings toward my own son,
whom I do love—or rather do want to love.

Saturday afternoon: Be it as it may, though, I love the boy
most dearly, & as I have been reading over what I have written,
I feel it rising higher & higher. Tell the little fellow about me.
I cannot bear to think that he cannot see me. He will not know
me. If I reckon right the 26th of June comes on Sunday & as that
is so near the 25th I think it will be well to have our Swinton
baptized, which will make a very interesting celebration of our
nuptials. My dear, I feel as if I know nothing of you.…

I have been busying myself around the house. I am working
in the closet in our room—4 drawers like those in father's closet
at Northampton. They are so convenient for clothing…I want
you to set down one thing—that our house is to be kept in <u>order</u>.
I hate to open a closet door & find every thing here and there,
which is too common a sight. I love order in a housekeeper.

Sabbath morn: Yes dear, I will tell you of my feelings. I fear
I love you too much, no not that I love you too much, but that I
love God too little. God is not in all my thoughts, but it seems as
if you are in all my thoughts, whether sleeping or waking. I seem
so utterly unfit to go to the Sanctuary and to administer at the
communion table.…

I am in as much distress as can be for your return, but I beg
that you would not hurry so as to take the least risk, for you are
too precious. In great haste, Affly your own E.

This is one of three letters from Erastus to Sarah, the only letters surviving that express his love as a husband to his wife. He is a man who loves passionately. His allusion to her "daily seat in my lap" and "the comfort they brought us," I read as a kind of lament for their sex life. He is working so hard to do what is right, to love God best of all because he is a man of his time, a time that relentlessly takes away the objects of your love.

He is tangled here between his love for his wife and his love for God. I think he's experiencing a momentary ebb in his faith, and I draw comfort from that, because I cannot seem to hold on to a faith myself that is not like a tide, coming in and going out.

He describes Beech Island as a gloomy place, truly in the backwoods. His concerns are not just for the landowners, but also for the slaves. He visits a sick slave woman and gives her a tract called "Poor Sarah." In the morning she is dead and he writes "you do not know how grateful I am that I was moved to do it; she is now beyond the reach of earthly good."

He passes the time doing domestic things, like building drawers in a closet, and just like my husband, makes an impassioned plea to his wife to be "orderly." I can see him bending in concentration, meticulously measuring boards for his drawers. I imagine him always in a white shirt with sleeves rolled, concentrating hard at whatever he is doing.

He writes in detail of purchasing the furniture for their home in Beech Island that will come, he laments, to $1000. It is a sizeable house with four bedrooms, a kitchen, dining room and parlor. His purchases include such items as a dozen chairs for $36, with caned seats and decoratively painted curved backs, "in the Grecian style" and straight legs. I have one that fits this description. Could it have been one of these twelve?

Her letters gush with a conventionally loving voice; she talks of her "spiritual awakening" and laments that the requirements of "propriety" keep her too bound to the conventions of Charleston society. In the furnishing of their house she is in charge of buying the feathers for the pillows, which cost 85 cents a pound, and the "paper" as in wallpaper. Their time in South Carolina is brief, for whatever reason. But by 1838, Sarah is writing letters to Charleston from Troy, New York, describing her life as a minister's wife ("received 19 people in the past few days, of all classes and walks of life"). I imagine that Erastus sought a church in the north to be closer to his ailing parents and a situation where he could finally live with his bride.

In my three days in Charleston I walk in the paths and to the places Sarah knew and Erastus visited. How comfortable was he at Bennettville, the great plantation house of her uncle the governor? Walking in the graveyard of St. Philips Episcopal Church I come upon a black guide giving a tour to a white southern couple. He stops mid-sentence to ask me if he can help me find a grave and we get into a conversation. I have just passed a Gadsden gravestone, Sarah's brother-in-law's name, and I tell him my puzzle. How could you be a genuine believer in Christ and still think it was all right to trade in human beings? With apologies for being an apologist, he tells me that these Englishmen had grown up with an idea that had evolved from feudal times: that to be able to own property was the true meaning of liberty. And slaves were just another type of property. He explains that they were able to hold two contradictory ideas in their heads: that this person in front of them was their property, and also Sam, or Maria, their "friend."

V

A Long Path to Tread in Bitterness and Alone

THE LAST FOLDER IN THE BOX IN SOUTH CAROLINA contains the poignant news of Sarah's death from pleurisy
at the end of her first year in Troy, at the moment her
daughter is born. Erastus's niece quotes a letter from him:

*Now it looks as though it was determined that the 2nd of May
hereafter should remind us of the Birthday of a Daughter, and
the 3rd of May while it leads the thoughts back to the birth of
my first born (Swinton's birthday) will also be bitterly dashed
in remembrance with the cup of affliction. Of Sarah's life there
is a bare hope. It is possible that a postscript to this letter may
inform you that she is no more. I a widower—& my children
motherless. All of us with the long path of life before us-to tread
in bitterness and alone.*

*She is now laboring under great oppression of the lungs,
and very short and quick breathing. She can say but little, and
that with great exertion. She is now too much occupied with her
pain and weariness to have any definite religious feelings. Her
remarks upon that subject, however, and her whole deportment
have indicated a sweet and calm frame of mind. 4 pm She is to
all appearance drawing near to death-calm-composed-happy-
not rapturous. She woke a few moments since from quite a
long refreshing nap. I said to her "you have had a sweet nap,*

my dear"-"Oh yes, she replied " a sweet nap"' "Try to go to sleep
again, if you sleep well perhaps God will yet spare you and us"
she replied "O my dear, presume not upon that."—She is now
asleep again. But we have no hope. Probably the next morning
will dawn upon her happy spirit in heaven.

Their baby daughter died soon after her mother. They had
named her Sarah.

This moment of death seizes my heart. If my father had
written such a letter about the dying of my mother, what would
it have said? What did he let himself feel? Did Erastus talk to
Swinton of this moment, later in his life? I am sure he told him
that Sarah had gone to heaven. What did that place look like in
little Swinton's imagination? I remember watching the ambu-
lance take my mother away as I stood next to my brother looking
through the screen of an open upstairs window. He was eight
and I was five. It was a hot August afternoon. The next morning
my father's best friend, my mother's doctor, came to the house
with his son who was my brother's age. We were eating jellied
orange slices out behind the garage, fat ones, covered in sparkles
of sugar. Westy said, "Your mother's dead." I said, "She is not."
And I ran screaming into the house. In my memory it was like
running into a deep dark hole.

Eventually my father remarried and the subject of my
mother, with her beautiful violet eyes, became explicitly forbidden. But shortly after he died forty years later I had an intense
desire to find the historical record, to know something of the
course of her disease. I remembered her hospital bed in our
house, but how long had she been in it? Had she been sick the
whole of my first five years? I mentally paced for days, working
up the courage to reach out and touch this ghost. And then one
day I punched in the number of the hospital and asked for Patient
Records. Did they have records that went that far back? I asked.

"You bet honey. If you want them, we'll copy them. What's
the patient's name?" As simple as that.

I went that afternoon and collected a six-inch packet of printed medical records in a white envelope and went home and closed myself in my room to read them. All typed on old fashioned typewritten hospital forms. Patient Name: Emerson, Margaret Drew, Occupation: Housewife, Age: 38; Color: White; Religion: Protestant; Sex: Female.

"Chief complaint: lumps in left breast of two months duration." "Family history: mother and father living; no history of tuberculosis, diabetes, heart disease, cancer, allergy or insanity." "Past history: measles, mumps, whooping cough and chicken pox. In 1918 she had the flu." Wow. She had survived the 1918 flu epidemic when she was nine years old. "Habits: one package of cigarettes a day. 2 cups of coffee. Takes alcohol only on social occasions and then in moderation. Weighs 125 pounds."

Then came the Operative Note: Biopsy left breast; left radical mastectomy. When the biopsy showed "adenocarcinoma," "the wound was closed with silk sutures, covered with gauze, and the field was reprepped and draped for a radical mastectomy. An elliptical incision…" …a scalpel was slicing off the top of my head, the page swam in front of me. Her blood pressure at her last hospital admittance on that August afternoon in 1952: 0 over 40. A curious little note said my father sponged a little Budweiser on her lips when she couldn't swallow.

The spring of the medical records, Hannah was a senior at Brown, an art major. She was taking a bookmaking course from professor and artist Walter Feldman. On Mother's Day she presented me with an exquisite grey linen boxed book. She had taken copies of the medical records and selected the most poignant and visually arresting pages. Transferring the images (typewritten forms, drawings and charts) onto creamy ridged vellum, she bound the folios into ten signatures. Each delicate folio of my mother's suffering she had hand-stitched with silver ribbon, and slid into place on the right hand side of the box. On the left side she had made an old fashioned photo album of Margaret's short life as a mother and wife, each photo held in place by black album corners on handmade paper, flecked with bits of flowers. On top of the whole was her "artist statement" which says "the handmade paper in this book was made from my mother's flannel nightie, cotton half-stuff, strong tea and flowers from an arrangement of my mother's." You can see this treasure in the collection of the John Hay Library at Brown, with a little piece of delicate paper on top that says "This book is a gift to my mother, Anne, on mother's day, 1995, in memory of Peggy, her mother." It's the cotton nightie that really gets me. That she has boiled down that soft old thing of mine and stirred and stirred and rolled it into paper—and impressed upon the paper the words and images that make me blind with my tears, this act of beauty is beyond me. She has bound the wounds of three generations in her "cotton half-stuff." In my mind I see us all standing tall together in our billowing nighties and for a moment I laugh at the image.

She made several of these books and gave one to my brother and one to me. I might never have looked again at my mother's medical records so wrenching was the experience that first time. But this exquisitely tender rendition enfolds me in my daughter's protective care and allows me to take a peek now and again at that darkest moment in my life.

★ ★ ★

I am back in my contemplation of Erastus's relationships. What if his first marriage had not ended prematurely? Would he have been such a spitfire if Sarah had lived? Would he have had his career as a leader of the Free Soil party and an active abolitionist? Did Sarah Bennett's memory and southern relatives become an awkwardness later in his life, the way my mother and her Canadian relatives became for my father, whose new wife demanded their banishment? I follow the thread of Erastus's life by calling the Rensselaer County Historical Society near Troy. A kind librarian, himself a leader in the local Presbyterian Church, sends me a packet of information on Erastus's sad time in Troy.

He was a popular minister but he left Troy in 1841 because of "illness and exhaustion." I will learn later that he had the "minister's malady:" bronchitis. I also receive in the mail a picture of a boyish Erastus, in a little oval among all the ministers who have served this Troy church. He is fair-haired and handsome with an expression that is sad and gentle. He is the only one on the page who is clean-shaven. His eyebrows rise in the center of his face like a little steeple, like Linc's sister Grace's. Like this great, great, great grandfather, whom she has never heard of, she is a student at the Andover Newton Theological Seminary.

Linc is diagnosed with schizophrenia a year into his incarceration. A violent crime is not unusual as a spur to diagnosing schizophrenia. Even before the diagnosis he has added his first assault to his murder charge. His parents had arranged for him to be evaluated at McLean Hospital. As they were sitting in a corridor waiting to be seen, a janitor with a bucket and mop backed into his mother by accident and Linc leapt at him like a pit bull, getting him in a head lock. His father wrestled him off. It would be the beginning of Linc's modest notoriety as a dangerous inmate.

Meanwhile, a North Carolina court gives him a sentence of six years for manslaughter. It was ruled that what had been an argument had turned into a deadly fight. With Linc by far the smaller of the two contestants, his lawyer argues self defense and plea bargains a six year sentence. But now Linc has new charges against him in Massachusetts. He can't start serving his manslaughter sentence until he has settled this new charge of assault. In the meantime he will be in solitary confinement for the next six years.

VI

Or Heaven Its Model

THE WEEK OF THE 2008 PRESIDENTIAL ELECTION I am in
North Carolina at the Duke Archives. I have discovered
through the internet that the papers of Erastus's son,
William Swinton Bennett Hopkins, have been deposited there.
Not exactly deposited but purchased by Duke in 1983 from a
dealer in Farmington, Connecticut. How did they come to be in
the hands of this dealer? Were they auctioned off as part of an
estate? Did a descendant in need decide to sell them?

This is my first trip to North Carolina. It's a state that could
vote either way and I wonder why I am diving into an archive
instead of campaigning for Obama. That is quickly revealed. Everyone here has made up their minds and is not speaking about
politics at all. Civility must reign. The only Republicans I know in
Boston are old line conservatives in their eighties. The kind they
have here are rare as blue-footed boobies in my world. I figure I
am just too late. Get on with the archives.

Since they were part of a commercial transaction, the papers
I have come to look at are quite well described in the summary
from the dealer's catalogue. They go from 1837 through the end
of the century and are described as relating to a family divided by
the Civil War. Swinton was part southerner, the only one in his
immediate family, just like my brother and I, part Canadian, are
foreigners relative to the rest of our Emerson clan.

All of my musings on our racist society and my dear Erastus's role in its making are rumbling through my brain like a slow mournful train as I sit in the Duke Archives on election day, 2008. It is without any doubt the most important election of my life and my absentee ballot is in. I am staying with a treasured former assistant who lives in a renovated tobacco factory in Raleigh and she is having an election party with all her young friends who have been fervently campaigning for months for Obama. Her parents are there and she truly doesn't know for whom they are voting because they won't tell her, but I know instantly. They are the sweet people who raised this wonderful woman, but it is simply beyond their ken to imagine a black man as President of the United States. They are very quiet as we all whoop and holler through the evening. North Carolina will be too close to call for weeks, but it finally will not matter.

I go out on the steps of the Duke Library the next morning, looking for cell phone reception. People are going about their business with none of the grinning and high-fiving that must be going on in Massachusetts. I look into each face that passes and wonder is this person miserable or joyous? I don't think there is any middle ground here but they are all being poker faced. Staring out at this very American, tranquil college quadrangle, I call my oldest daughter Jody. She starts to cry. "I realized last night Mom, that this is the first moment of my life I have ever been proud to be an American." She is thirty-seven.

Erastus went back to Northampton in 1841 and married Charlotte Freylinghuesen Allen. The marriage was recorded by Judge William Allen, D.D., her father, who slyly notes in the margin of the record that this was his daughter he had married. He was president of Dartmouth and Bowdoin Colleges in his career, having married Maria Malleville Wheelock, the granddaughter of the founder of Dartmouth. Now I know why my little correspondent in Box 4 carries the weighty name of Malleville. Charlotte and Erastus came back from their honeymoon and settled into the house on King Street that his father, John, had built in 1824. John would die the next year at 72 and his wife Lydia would live on with them to see the birth of their first two children. Charlotte's parents lived five houses down on King Street. The generations were deeply intertwined.

I have one letter from Lydia, Erastus's mother, written to Sarah Bennett when Swinton is born. I paused at this passage:

When my first born was but a few days old Father Hopkins [this must have been Erastus's grandfather] *during one of his daily visits, begged me to establish one firm, undeviating rule with the babe which was to begin then, that day: which was: that I would never make a promise to the child til I was ready to fulfill it., observing how wrong it was of mothers (for that is often the way), when the child gave symptoms of hunger to say "you shall have your way, my babe.", then wishing to finish something she may have in hand, the child is put off. The poor child grows more uneasy and she renews the promise, but keeps on with her work, til for peace sake she is obliged to fulfill her promise. Then he gave me the faithful charge never to promise til I was ready to fulfill it." Adding "you must regard your own word in all things and then the babe will soon learn that mother's word may be depended upon; and in this way the child will be taught from its birth to speak the truth. For the reverse will teach the child to lie.*

I love this simple, earnest piece of child raising advice. It is so far removed from the moral confusion we live in now. This is an eighteenth-century woman, born into a time and family that aspired to an absolute kind of truth and purity. They faced real threats to their daily existence and believed that godly behavior was all that would protect them. We have been almost entirely delivered from threats to our daily life. And what would Lydia think about what have we done with this gift?

Erastus's second wife must have been "the girl next door" during his adolescence. Did he return home to Northampton, a widower with a small boy and revisit an earlier relationship? Widowers with small children have a real incentive to marry quickly, but there is lots of evidence that this was also a marriage of love. My father had been left in similar straits, with two children, five and eight years old, and it wasn't a pretty picture. He was sad and distracted. He gained weight and lost his hair. He buried himself in his work and was the subject of intensive matchmaking efforts by his friends. A series of strange women took my brother and me on the Swan Boats in the Public Garden trying to woo our affections. Grandparents descended upon our household to cook and sew and make us take naps. My father most of all wanted to find a woman who would do a competent job of raising his children so he could concentrate on his cortisone research. He found a widow with three children of her own. Her husband had been killed in a plane crash. Her name was Betty Davis. I thought he meant the movie star. They were married six weeks after they met.

1841 was for Erastus a watershed moment in his life, not just because he remarried, but because he gave up the ministry. Like all men in the very tiny class of educated New Englanders of his time, his education had been overwhelmingly religious. The only college degree was a Doctor of Divinity. His education would have been intense in its discipline, starting with daily prayers in his family as soon as he could talk.

But it was a trying time to be the shepherd of a flock. Many congregations were divided over holding on to old orthodoxies or moving to a more direct spiritual communion with God. Ralph Waldo Emerson resigned his post as minister of the Second Church in Boston in 1832 because he did not believe any more in giving communion. He was ill and tired and he sailed to Europe. Erastus made the same break and the same trip, taking his new wife Charlotte to Rome on their honeymoon in 1841. One of his last acts as a clergyman was to write a small volume titled *The*

Family, a Religious Institution or Heaven Its Model, published in Troy in 1840 and waiting for me in the stacks of Widener Library. It is an examination of the institution of the family in the Bible and declares it one of God's fundamental creations, "fixed like the foundations of the earth and the bounds of the sea." So it is not entirely surprising that Erastus marries again at this moment and has seven more children whom he carefully nurtures in the love and understanding of God, while he cares for his aging parents.

I am sure there were plenty of bad marriages in Erastus's time. The parental love that makes us secure in our own capacities to love was much more likely to be interrupted in a world with no antibiotics and limited medical knowledge. Maybe the all-encompassing religious faith of some in that time filled those voids with God's love. A kind of love triangle. But I bet there were still plenty of marriages like the first one that I made back in the sixties, when convention dictated that women should get married after college, ready or not. Thrashing around for someone to save me from adulthood, I married a much older man, whose horrific childhood filled me with a compassion that I mistook for love. I was fiercely determined to love him, no matter what. But at twenty-three my ability to imagine time rolling out slowly in decades before me was as limited as my ability to imagine real love.

My children were born of that first marriage, a marriage that was such an astonishing mismatch that I have always felt it was ordained only so that they could come into being. It is the kind of self-soothing thought that goes through the mind of many who make drastic mistakes in marriage. We were divorced when our girls were five and eight, the ages exactly of my brother and me when our mother died. As if I were working through that loss all over again through them. I was ready this time. I asked him to leave, and when he showed no signs of doing so, I invited the sheriff to come and deliver the papers to him.

Our children spent alternate weekends with their father, but they slept at Ruthie and Mark's house, their lives intertwined with Linc's and the two girls. Our daughters have grown up to be artists. Jody is a ceramic sculptor and Hannah a conceptual artist who does installations. Art is a way of working through things.

★ ★ ★

The change Erastus made in his life was radical, from leading a congregation with all of the petty politics and handholding that can entail, to an active life of regional politics and development. He became president of the Connecticut River Railroad just as the first tracks were being laid, and a passionate spokesman of the Free Soil Movement against the extension of slavery into the west. His active commuting life, in service to the Free Soil movement and his constituents, had the precious result that he wrote to his children, and unbeknownst to him, to his great-great grandchildren. I have now figured out the obvious: when there are no letters for a period of time, it's because everyone's at home.

We all remarried in the prime of our lives, Erastus, my father and I. My father and Betty took their newly acquainted brood of five children with them on their weekend honeymoon in Lake Placid, New York, where my new stepbrother Mat was being redeposited in his boarding school, a small homey place that specialized in traumatized children. Why did my father think this woman would be such a wonderful mother?

Peter and I went on our honeymoon to Rome in 1992 and I imagine it was not so different from Erastus and Charlotte's trip. They would have had a long passage on a sailing ship. We took the eight-minute water shuttle ride to the Boston airport at four in the afternoon and were in Rome by morning. They would have stayed near the Forum or the Pantheon, maybe even in the Hotel Portuguesi where we stayed, or its predecessor. The Forum would have looked almost the same in 1841 as it did in 1992, though recently it has been fenced in so you can no longer amble through it.

Erastus bought Charlotte a cameo angel pin in Rome. Fifty years later their daughter Sallie described it in an inventory of her mother's jewelry. "It was beautifully cut and Papa took much pride in it and often exhibited it using the magnifying glass which I find now [March 1891] in his secretary. This was her chief ornament until 1864. Then she put on a jet cross with gold tips, and a jet pin with a pearl in the center."

I thought a lot about marriage in the first few years of the new millenium, with two daughters struggling to find the right mate and my own still far away. I was living alone in our big house in Boston, waiting for Peter's seven-year contract in Kansas City to end. Sometimes I turned on the Red Sox game on the radio to conjure his presence. We both hated the telephone. Our grown up daughters were off loving their independence and not in need of me at the moment. America was starting a war with the wrong country. It was not a happy time. But I got to know myself in the way you're supposed to know yourself before you get married in the first place.

I read once long ago that we pick a mate who both has qualities we were in some way denied in our childhood, but also represents some unfinished business with our parents. The missing qualities that I gained when I married Peter were two in particular: the ability to soak up beauty directly from its source, and to have guiltless fun. In my extended Emerson family shingling the roof together was considered quite enough fun for a day. And one should be practical in selecting a honeymoon destination, and a wife.

It was impossible to imagine my father tramping from church to church in Rome searching for special altarpieces or standing in front of a Michelangelo *Pieta* for an hour or two. But my husband could lead me endlessly on these beautiful scavenger hunts. One year we drove through Bavaria hunting down Rococo churches. Places like Chartres in France spoke of an austere love of God, but these small churches were like special desserts made in his honor, giant whipped cream structures with voluptuous white and gilded angels in every corner. Between churches we would stop in some Bavarian village restaurant, have a pint or two, a few potatoes and sausages, and move on to the next stop.

Peter picked Valentine's Day to get married—not only for its romantic value but also for its proximity in the calendar to the President's Day holiday—which we stretch every year to a week of hedonistic pleasure. In Venice one year, lugging a very heavy art book, we made a special scavenger hunt for altarpieces. In the thin February sunlight we would plow along in the Vaporetto to whatever little neighborhood church was on our list. We were almost always alone, standing in front of an astonishing creation, four hundred years old. Sometimes we would find the whole thing intact, the painting by Bellini, the sculpted altar by some other astonishing talent. We would have the awesome feeling that we were the first ones ever to see this. Then our craving for another wonderful Italian lunch would move us to go blinking back out into the sunshine to look for our *primo* and *secondo* (a pasta and a little piece of meat) and maybe some *insalata* and some *vino*. Not so different from what the artists ate four hundred years before, though I am sure we eat a lot more of it now.

These little trips were a tribute to the idea that the more you learn about something, the greater the pleasure you get from it. And to the idea that a lifetime spent with a good partner exponentially expands your view of the world, even if you have to survive a few rough patches. I am sorry that I have no letters from Erastus telling us what he saw in Rome. All the same altarpieces were there, most in the same places. And I am sorry I have no letters from him advising his children on marriage. The closest I get is this letter to his father-in-law on the gift of Charlotte. I can picture him sitting down at the desk in his study with Creamy the dog, maybe a Golden Lab, curled up by his feet. His hair is a sandy gray and he has his white shirt on, sleeves rolled up, grey vest and black pants. Head bent in concentration. It is his 25th wedding anniversary and he is fifty-six years old.

Letter to Grandpa Allen
N. Bridgeton, Nov 18, 1866

My Dear Sir,

It is 25 years since, this very eveg, that I rec'd from your hands, and with your blessing, the gift of your daughter. My experience with her for one quarter of a century has been such that it is but a just tribute to say that in her the scripture hath been fulfilled and that her price has been far above sublime. The heart of her husband has safely trusted in her; she has done him good and not evil all the days of her life; she has opened her heart with wisdom and in her tongue has been the balm of kindness; her children have risen up and called her blessed; her husband also, and he praiseth her. And I have only to add, in address to her "Many daughters have done virtuously, but thine excellest them all.

"A prudent wife is from the Lord." First of all and above all, thanks are due to Him. But I cannot but feel a debt of gratitude to that noble and virtuous mother that bore her and imparted so much of her own reputed sweetness–and to you who reared her, and blessed her with your own hands as you gave her to me.

Your affectionate son, Erastus Hopkins

The letter speaks not only of his wife and marriage, but its somewhat archaic biblical tone suggests the respect and reverence in which he holds his father-in-law, who lives just five doors down the street. It is impossible to imagine such a letter being written today. Modern psychology has given us the dubious ability to describe most behavior as some kind of pathology, good or bad. We see the holes in people and attribute them to some lack in their upbringing. Rare is the person who would think of their spouse as their gift from God. Peter rejects all my amateur psychologizing and is ambivalent about God. He sees the world in terms of archetypal narratives. His plays are his therapy, and since he gets to pick each one, their themes are the themes of our lives together and the universal themes of our world.

I wonder now where Charlotte's cameo pin is. Perhaps in the jewelry box of a descendent, or maybe I saw it in a shop window on State Street. Now I look around at the furniture that has passed down to me. My beautiful bow-fronted bureau with Annette Hopkins written on an old red bordered sticker in my grandmother's hand, was surely in Erastus's house on King Street. Now Peter's shirts and sweaters are nested neatly inside; maybe it was Erastus's, full of his shirts, and socks and handkerchiefs, the little intimate things of life.

VII

A Companion in Our Circle

IN A SEEMING BLINK OF AN EYE Jody, my oldest daughter has fallen in love, married, and most miraculously given birth to an astonishingly beautiful son. As if to follow in a family tradition, both of my cousin Ruthie's daughters, Grace and Allie, have also just been delivered of healthy babies. They will be a triumvirate at the communion rail in the chapel in no time. I am invited to be present in the delivery room and almost hold my breath for her seven hours of labor for fear of disturbing her fierce concentration or my unimaginable good fortune. Her husband Andrew and her doula are coaching her. At one point the doctor comes in and pulls Andrew aside. Later Andrew tells me with a giggle that she was asking if they wanted me in the delivery room. "I have two patients in labor and one of them told me under no circumstances should I let her mother in, and now I can't remember which one it was," the doctor had confessed.

Being the mother of a loving adult woman is very unfamiliar territory. My childhood relationship to my stepmother was harsh; my adult relationship with her was distant and fearful. Now my daughter passes the tiny bundle that is her son into my arms and I find myself stunned to be in this circle of light and love. Suddenly my cup has gone from empty to full. Peter is still in Kansas City but his contract will end soon. I drive to Brooklyn in the early dawn to the tiny fourth floor walkup in which my grandson will begin his life and start to bake and clean in a celebratory frenzy.

When his first grandchild, named for his first wife, Sarah, is born, Erastus writes a letter to Swint full of happy humor. He starts by saying: "The welfare of parents, their peace & happiness is largely involved in the conduct of their children. Of this, your experience is to come; the dawn is even now."

Returning home from Brooklyn after a fortnight I turn my attention to Northampton. I have discovered that the archives of the Museum hold two boxes of Erastus's family papers. I set out on the Mass Pike one morning, climbing the hundred mile rise carved by a glacier millions of years ago. Amherst and Northampton were the seat of my grandparents' courtship and my grandfather's childhood home, so they have long been part of my mythic landscape. But I have never done more than pass through them. I come into the town, pass the cemetery and search for King Street where I've figured out from insurance maps the Hopkins home stood. It is now a garish strip of fast food restaurants and gas stations with a Catholic church and parish house where Erastus's house would have been. But the railroad depot is still there and I can see where the tracks ran behind the site of the house.

The block of Bridge Street that is my destination is almost unchanged from the nineteenth century. The Museum is in a small clapboard house wrapped in a collection of white New England farm buildings. I walk up the curved brick pathway planted with early spring perennials. The sun is beating down, the bees are drowsily feeding and I feel time unwinding. I am being anointed with that slow spirit of patience that is required in the deciphering of handwriting in old letters.

The boxes sit waiting for me in a cozy little workroom, shared by the Museum's staff. The atmosphere is a striking counterpoint to the formality of the Massachusetts Historical Society. The finding-aid is detailed enough to direct me immediately to the correspondence that most interests me: Erastus's own letters. These are dated earlier than those held by the MHS. I open the folder and begin to read. The first is a letter to that same father-in-law to whom he was so grateful for his wife, but this one is eighteen years earlier.

Northampton, April 9, 1848 Sabbath

My Dear Father,

Charlotte and the babe are very well. You know the tale of joy—that one week since I came home to the birth of a fine daughter, under every circumstance of joy. The children were delighted; we were all happy.

I returned again last evening at 7 pm. When I arrived at the depot all were well, happy, full of life under my roof. But before I reached my house, the scene changed. I entered my door eager to embrace my children, when notes of distress met my ear. They were the preludes of death. This Sabbath morning, just one week after the birth of a child, I was called to look upon the lonely form of a departed child—yea more, a departed son— my own, my sweet Willie. Spare, spare your sorrows, my dear Father, for you I know, you will weep. Yet the event, awful and sudden as it is, is none the less true. That name "Willie" which has signified to us so much of life and endearment, is now the token of our sorrows—it is the talisman of our tears! The sun of yesterday set upon his life, (oh how perfect and joyous!); the sun of this day rose upon his death. And we are bathed in tears—we are of prostrate strength—we are sunken in affliction. But we do not murmur. The Lord gave and the Lord has taken. It was a precious gift—oh how precious and beautiful! You know well. It came from the bosom of God, we have returned it to the bosom of Jesus. Rest, rest there, my darling boy, and be at rest. Jesus' love is tenderer, stronger than ours. For thy highest, perfect joy we are willing to pay the price of our bitter anguish! He was here blithe and happy for a little while, and has already passed the only trial of his existence.

The last words he uttered, as in a state of apparent unconsciousness, as he stretched upward his little hands, were "I want to go and see Grandmama." A few minutes more and he was where she is. Did the spirit speak to him? Was the veil lifted from his vision? Blessed boy! He cannot come to us, we must go to him. Shall we see him in our dying hours? Will he be heaven's messenger to lead us up to God?

It was a sad and fearful accident that changed his joy into pain—his life (so full) into death. After two hours intense suffering from the effects of scalding water which covered more than half the surface of his body, including the stomach and the bowels, he fell asleep and seemed comparatively quiet and easy, til he died within a few moments of a week from the birth of the babe which he loved so much.

His last hours of suffering were spent upon his mother's sight, as she lay upon her bed. A child beginning life on one side, and a child ending life on the other! Was not this joy and sorrow in the same cup?

The first voice of a living child which met our ears this morning was the birdlike Caro saying "all gone." The voice and the sentiment! How full of meaning! Every sight and every sound of our living children remind us of the sight and sound that have passed away. There is a companion wanting in their circle—there is a note wanting in their harmony.

He now lies under the glass in the north room. We hoped to have had you here at the burial, but we are advised to have it this P.M.

We long to see you. Charlotte is as composed as she can be— as any mother can be—but oh it racks her soul.

In haste, your affectionate son, Erastus

I grow icy cold reading this letter. Looking at the two librarians plodding through their work beside me, I feel as if I am in another time and climate zone. I look through the papers I had copied at the New England Historical and Genealogical Society and find the list of Erastus and Charlotte's children. Though I had read the dates in the family genealogy, I had not really taken in the mortality in this list. Now I encounter in a visceral way the brutal blow a child's death strikes. The Hopkins Genealogy lists the following children of this second marriage:

> Sarah Anna, b. September 1842; d. 11 February 1930 at the
>   age of 87. Residence Northampton; unm. (Sally) (87 years)
> Maria Malleville, b. 23 August, 1843; d 1 September 1843.
> William Allen, b. 2 January 1845; d 9 April 1848. (Willie)
> Caroline Dwight, b 24 June 1846; d 21 July 1864. (Caro)
> Mary Annette, b. 2 April 1848; d 31 August 1897. (Nettie)
> Charlotte Freylinghuysen, b. 1 October, 1849; d. 28 May
>   1856. (Lottie)
> John b. 29 September 1850; d. 18 May, 1856. (Johnnie)

I am flooded with the bright image of my newborn grandson, of his preciousness above all things in my life. Erastus must have gone through all the same stages with Willie that I am soon to go through with Eamon: following him endlessly up and down the stairs as he learns to negotiate them, playing hide and seek, seeing that magical grin of astonished revelation.

Erastus would have written this letter at a writing desk a stone's throw from where I sit, with sun streaking in the upper panes of the window, just as it is doing here in this little house a hundred and sixty years later in the same week in April. His hand must have been heavy and slow, the brightness of the day invisible to him.

I find a little snippet in a southern newspaper that describes what happened. It was Saturday night and boiling water for a bath had been put in a tub. Willie, with all the exuberance of a little boy, my own dear boy, must have jumped into it. His mother was lying-in with her newborn, his father coming back from Boston on the train, and a servant girl probably in charge of him—or perhaps Swinton or Sally. I am in the grip of this terrible grief.

Later in the afternoon I go to the cemetery a few blocks away and find the family plot. There they are: Erastus and Charlotte in front. Four little graves in back, and Caroline, Mary Annette and Sarah in the first row with their parents. The headstones are all white marble, worn and spotted with yellow and black lichen. The cemetery is dilapidated, the headstones a little askew.

I feel at home in cemeteries. They are lovely, quiet places and they are packed with history. I go often to visit my mother's grave and feel as if I am entering a separate kingdom where the animals rule. The red-tailed hawk sits perfectly still on a headstone nearby and watches me. A red fox trots by as if I am not there at all. My mother's monument has an art nouveau flourish that pleases me and I wonder who chose it. My father? My grandmother or my aunt? An old black and white snapshot, the kind with scalloped edges, shows us standing beside it, my father, my brother, and me holding on to each other, looking a little unsteady. I am grinning a toothless six-year-old smile looking like I'm hoping that if I smile hard enough it will somehow hold us up, keep us together. When my father died fifty years later the cemetery plot came to me and I pay each year for the care of the two azaleas on either side of the headstone. My grandparents are buried there too. I thought that Peter and I would join them someday, but the other day he said that he imagined himself flying on the wind, not being buried. I am reminded of my friend Katia who at ninety-six is arguing passionately with her daughter on this question. Her daughter is a Hasidic Jew and her belief system doesn't allow for cremation. Katia gets a claustrophic panic just thinking about being closed up in a box and put in the ground. They are at an impasse. Her daughter weeps at the thought that there would be no grave to visit, no place to sit by her mother. I am torn. Sitting by my mother has restored my soul over the years but I admit that I like the vaguely scientific idea that the molecules of my body would be released in the wind to become a tiny part of a billion new things. I will trust my soul to God.

No one is caring anymore for these worn and mossy marble headstones in this Bridge Street Cemetery in Northampton. I am surely the first who has passed by in many years who knows who these people were. We will all be forgotten in the end, but might someone in the meantime make new meaning of our lives in some distant time of their own?

The husband of my dear friend Jean died recently. I fly to Natchitoches, Louisiana to visit her. She is a classics professor at the Scholars College of Northwestern State University and we have been friends for thirty years. I have been telling her of my discovery of the Erastus letters and she is excited, thinking I am writing a scholarly history of his life. I don't know quite how to tell her that I have been moved in a different direction, by a spirit that took me completely by surprise. She adamantly does not believe in God. I sit on her porch under the huge Magnolia trees and listen to her banging around in the kitchen. In my mind's eye I can see her tiny frame with her slightly bent shoulders, her mouth a straight line of sober concentration. She has taught me a lot about friendship over the years and I feel helpless now in the face of this loss of hers. We have never been chatty together: our friendship burns through the long pauses of our conversation. Now I feel the void in her heart; it pulls me in. I've been dreaming terrible dreams since I arrived. I do not know if there is any comfort in my presence.

We go to the cemetery and to the funeral home to select a headstone. We stand over her husband's freshly dug grave, the red Louisiana soil like a wound in the earth. I find myself getting all businesslike, looking around the cemetery for suitable examples of doubles and singles, as they call them. Should it be red granite or grey? Rough edged or smooth? He was a librarian. All she wants for sure is an open book inscribed in Latin on the tombstone. An hour later we are driving along in silence, lost in the backwoods of Louisiana. I realize that fussing over the headstone selection has provided a short respite to feeling. What splendid defenses a mind has.

In my travels to Amherst and Northampton I have visited other family graves in addition to the Hopkins family. My great grandfather, Nettie's husband, is buried in the Wildwood Cemetery, next to the Dickinson plot. Emily Dickinson's parents were slightly older than Charlotte and Erastus and they knew each other well. Emily would have been eighteen when Willie died and his death would surely have moved her. I am told by historian Bruce Laurie that "Erastus loathed Edward for his undying loyalty to the Whig Party which Erastus left in 1848 because of its refusal to oppose the expansion of slavery," and that they were competitors in the development of the railroad. "I like to see it lap the miles and lick the valleys up," Emily wrote of the locomotive. Edward strangely encouraged his wife and daughter to visit the state lunatic asylum in Worcester which I can only imagine was because he was engaged with Erastus in the campaign to develop the Northampton Asylum. Edward's political career ended abruptly in the splintering of the Whig and Free Soil parties and the rise of the Know-Nothing Party.

Emily was steeped in the same fervent religious culture that emanates from Erastus's letters to his own daughters. She was the object of many prayer circles hoping for her salvation, her surrender to God. She had a brief moment in her early teens when she felt that comfortable conversational presence of the Lord, but then she lost it. Later she said, those "few short moments...I would not now exchange for a thousand worlds like this. It was then my greatest pleasure to commune alone with the great God & to feel that he would listen to my prayers." Great artists are not usually cut from comfortable religious cloth. They are born of struggle and her poems are full of an entirely original and personal spiritual life. The hiddenness of her self and her poetry, sewn up by her own careful hand in booklets and secreted away, seems almost like a game—awaiting discovery. She played with it. "I am nobody. Who are you? Are you nobody too?"

In the attic of grandfather Kendall's house in Maine there is an old leather album that my brother and I would reverently dig out every summer. Tucked inside are three little letters from Emily Dickinson. The words shimmered off the paper as we read them aloud.

Dear Kendall, Christmas in Bethlehem means most of all this year. Our Santa Claus still asks the way to Gilbert's little friends. Is Heaven an unfamiliar road? Come sometime with your sled and tell Gilbert's. Aunt Emily (Christmas 1883)

The next one reads: *Missing my own boy I knock at other trundle beds, and trust the Curls are in—Little Gilbert's Aunt* (Christmas 1884)

And finally: *Dear Kendall, I send you a Blossom with my love—spend it as you will—The woods are too deep for your little feet to grope for Evergreen—Your friend Emily* (Christmas, 1885)

Kendall was Nettie's little boy—Nettie who was born the week that Willie died. Her son was my grandfather and his best boyhood friend was Emily Dickinson's beloved nephew, Gilbert. He lived in the Evergreens, the house next door to Emily's Homestead and a short run through the woods to Kendall's house. In 1883 the two eight-year old boys were playing in a mud puddle together and both contracted typhoid fever. Gilbert died. Kendall lived. Gilbert's room in the Evergreens remains just as it was in that year with a little blue velvet suit laid out on the bed. Emily was distraught at her beloved nephew's death and each year at Christmas gave little Kendall a gift with these notes. "Is heaven an unfamiliar road?" Emily's poetry and these delicate notes hold that void so tenderly. No other voice has ever quite achieved it. In it I hear an echo of Erastus's lamentations for his lost children. I think there is a glimmering thread of heaven between these two. It catches me.

On one of my visits to Amherst I found the original notes in Emily's hand, given by my grandfather to the Amherst College Archive. They have the physical beauty of Japanese calligraphy;

her script looks like gentle waves lapping on the page. The notes whisper of the last three Christmas seasons of her life, times when she was full of physical and emotional suffering and writing little. The last one comes months before her death May of 1886.

We are living in the fall of the swine flu and I am fearful for my grandchildren, though it is a miniscule fear compared to what Erastus must have felt. We have come so far in our conquest of microbes that the threat seems very dim. We are literally grasping for immortality and who knows, maybe if we pay enough, it will be ours one day. Will heaven be an unfamiliar road?

For Erastus immortality was about the grace of being taken into God's kingdom and his fear was not that his children would die, but that they would not go to heaven. In his letters to Nettie and Caro I see the way he strives to prepare them to be among the anointed. As he suffers Willie's death, he is given, almost in the same moment, the new life of his daughter Mary Annette, as though God were apologizing for taking his precious boy.

The grief seems never-ending. Two more children, Charlotte and John, are born shortly after Nettie in 1849 and 1850. Years earlier on my first day in the first folder, I had a hint of the sadness to come in cousin Willie Smith's little smudged note asking if Johnnie had been buried in the garden or the cemetery. There are no more letters I can find that say what the fate of these children are, so I go up to the Hampshire County Courthouse and look in the book that records marriages, births and deaths. Johnnie and Lottie died in 1856 in May, ten days apart, of Scarlet Fever, a virulent killer in the nineteenth century before antibiotics. Along with Maria Malleville, the first baby of Charlotte and Erastus, their brief lives and Willie's, are marked by the four small white marble headstones in the Northampton cemetery. Charlotte's diary has poignant notations of her anniversary visits to each of these little graves every year until her own passing in 1890.

VIII

*...Freedom must and will prevail while
slavery will wear away*

I RECEIVE AN EMAIL FROM MY COUSIN GRACE, Linc's sister, my
goddaughter. Of all the members of my family she is the one
whose eyes look out at me when I see pictures of Erastus,
whose bright heart shines from Nettie's letters. She is a student
at Andover Newton Theological School, where Erastus went in
1832. Did he beckon her down that path?

Her email to our extended family asks us to send letters
to Linc. He has been in isolation in prison for five years and is
acutely lonely. Would we write? He is at last on medication that
controls his schizophrenia sufficiently to make it possible to communicate with him. His time in prison has been punctuated with
explosions of violence when his medications are not adjusted
properly, or he decides not to take them.

I feel that cool lurch of the heart, that feeling you get when
you know what's right but you can't for the life of you imagine
actually doing it. My mind shuts like a seized engine when I try to
think of a first sentence. It's been years since I wrote a real letter.
I walk around for a few days trying to push this request out of my
mind, but it keeps slipping back, until finally the man who wrote
letters every day comes to my mind. Maybe Erastus did the work
a hundred and fifty years ago and I just have to do a little weaving.

So I write to Linc and tell him about his great-great-great
grandfather, about my trail of discovery and how I feel like he was
writing to me. Who knows, maybe Linc will find some comfort

in this voice and in thinking of the embrace of generations that stand behind him. I suggest that if Erastus were alive he would be writing beautiful letters to Linc and giving him every encouragement. Mine are paltry efforts in comparison but I send them with the same spirit. I copy a couple of Erastus's letters into my own for Linc, hoping that maybe he'll want to know more. The irony of the fact that we're both hearing voices is not lost on me.

I have found another trove of materials through Widener Library at Harvard. From the sanctuary of the reference room, I can electronically access the full text of nineteenth century newspaper articles and search a vast database for news of Erastus. I find that one hundred and forty-one articles mention him in some way. I begin the slow process of loading each one and reading the news article in its original format. It is a thrilling process of suspense and discovery, organized chronologically so that I am following Erastus's life, a kind of bell curve of activity, trickling reports at the beginning and the end, but a flood in the middle. I contemplate my own bell curve and realize that I am on my way down on the arc, but that I probably have a ways to go. Erastus died at the age I am right now.

For seven years I have been a reader in Erastus's intimate circle, listening to his voice of love and comfort as he scribbles tender notes to his children, charting them through the shoals of adolescence. Here in these newspaper accounts is the public man.

The trickle begins with a report of the young Erastus giving the "forenoon oration" at the Dartmouth College commencement in 1830. Then Garrison's complaint of "Presbyterian ministers marrying into slaveholding families" in *The Liberator* in 1836. I will eventually learn that in the 1850s his Northampton home was a stop on the Underground Railroad and that he was an active agent. But at the age of twenty-three he is the author of the annual report of the American Colonization Society whose purpose was to send freed blacks back to Africa to evangelize (and get out of America). As I search for an understanding of Erastus's relationship to slavery, I have to acknowledge that the vast majority of Northerners were not in favor of abolitionism. Most northerners were simply seeking a path to rapprochement with the South and considered abolitionism a radical and destructive route. But there are hints in Erastus's writings about the Colonization Society that he is engaged in a kind of fifth column activity.

To quote his own words: "[The Colonization Society's] sole and simple object is to colonize the free people of colour with their own consent. All unite in this. As they proceed, and the colony grows, and the subject assumes importance, a door seems to be opened; thoughts of emancipating slaves occur;...And while keeping quietly and silently at its one simple object, it finds discussions of abolition arising up, and the spirit of emancipation extending, where but a little while before, it was treason to lisp it." This was exactly the kind of subversion that South Carolinians were afraid of with the Colonization Society, so it is startling to hear him express it so directly.

Whatever one thinks of his arguments, they are eloquently stated by a very young man. (He was twenty-three.) Life was a short and serious business in those days and the teenager hadn't been invented. You were raised to do God's work. The other attachments that would come were of this world and were transient—what Erastus would have called momentary reflections of God. This knowledge was transmitted from generation to generation, through prayer, conversation and letters. The sense of a rightly ordered life was meticulously instilled. All those confusing pathways of desire that so clamor for our daily attention (television, cell phones, the internet) had yet to be invented. You had time then, to go deeply into things. Parents knew exactly what they wanted to see develop in their child and they were not shy about nurturing it. At Harvard I also find that little volume that Erastus published in 1841: *The Family, a Religious Institution or Heaven Its Model.* He must have been writing it just before Sarah died when his world came crashing down. It leaves no doubt that he had meditated on the stages of parenthood and what needed to be imparted at each moment. It is a roadmap of responsibility. Holding my first beautiful infant at her moment of birth I had not a clue, just raw human instinct and overwhelming love to guide me. Erastus started writing to Nettie when she was just five. He told her a story, a sweet mini-sermon.

February 1, 1854 from Cleveland

Dear Nettie

I was coming out of the Post Office the other evening and saw a little girl about as big as you. She was poor. And she was looking on the sidewalk and was crying. I asked her what was the matter. She sobbed and said "I have lost my three cents." I asked her what she was going to do with her three cents. She cried and said "Mother gave them to me to buy some soda biscuits for the baby." I loved the little girl when I heard her speak so of her mother and of the baby. I had ten cents and I gave them all to her. I thought if you had been there you would have given her some of your cents. Would You?

Your dear Papa

We struggle now, to know what to say to our children. We fear their attachment to us is not strong enough to bear our entreaties, that they will reject us entirely. We have an astonishing array of tools to communicate, but they all seem wanting when something serious needs to be said, and pondered by the recipient. Direct conversation is difficult when the pace of life doesn't hand us easy quiet moments. The music is usually blaring, and now television has even invaded that once promising space for conversation, the car. Emails are about brevity and our index finger hovers over the red x for delete. Letters do not sit in our heart waiting to be written anymore, they are a chore. We write them without grace and wit because we're not in that habit. If you get one you fear that it may contain news too difficult to say out loud.

Meanwhile our minds are being bent like birches by messages over which we have no control. I am reminded of a wonderful new Greek word I have just learned from a Catholic friend: *logismoi*—the tendency to be led astray, even assaulted, by thoughts—from the path of virtue. I read today of teenage girls who are forming support groups to help each other log on to Facebook only once a month. Can a whole country be afflicted by *logismoi*?

In Erastus's house the evenings would have been spent together. The tedious work of maintaining oil lamps dictated that only a few would be lit in the evening and the family would gather in one room together. They would sit in quiet conversation, play games, sing or do individual projects like sewing or writing. Once the electric light and central heating were invented everyone went off to their own rooms, no doubt luxuriating in the silence but also retreating from intimacy and conversation.

Erastus would be astonished to witness my struggle at letter writing, but surely proud to see his own words put to such good use. I wonder if he was a gadget man, like my father, and would have delighted in the computer and all of its progeny. He would be stunned to see what has replaced intimacy in this generation, the instant access his great-great-grandchildren have to all of their friends at once. What is the currency of friendship now? Has it been devalued or multiplied? I read that teenagers fear intimacy. I don't suppose it was a word Erastus used much, it was just there in his world, by necessity—the basis of the power of his words to his children. It is this intimacy I am borrowing from Erastus as I write to Linc. I cannot conjure it on my own. In our time we long for it, and we fear it. Like many very uncomfortable trends, this one is being articulated by artists.

I read in *The Boston Globe* that the Foster Prize in contemporary art has just been awarded to Andrew Witkin. I sit up and pay attention because I know him: he was my daughter's boyfriend for a year and a half—a member of our family. The work that won this prize is described as "an uncanny installation of fastidiously arranged personal effects and impersonal furniture that he calls "Untitled 1990—" blurring the separation between arts and life. The overall effect is strangely haunting, at once crowded with memory and desire and devastatingly empty." The Institute of Contemporary Art's director describes it as "evoking simultaneously a sense of isolation and a longing for connection."

My daughter is also an artist. She abstracts the events and interactions she records among people in different situations into colorful ribbons and flags and knots: beautiful but distancing the observer one more step from whatever intimacy may have been in the original moment. Her installations have their own floating beauty and suggest a secret code to another ephemeral reality.

My imagination is suddenly seized with an image of Erastus coming to Hannah's opening. They would make their way toward each other from across the room, guided by some magnetic force of recognition. He would tuck her arm under his and smile appreciatively at the startling ganglions of ribbon and tape rising out of the floor and coming down from the ceiling. Strange as it would at first seem to him, he would get it in a rush of intuition. He would see the serious quest in her life, and he would see God's light in her, and in her work. And she would earnestly begin to explain to him the way in which everything has multiple meanings in the world and that you can intertwine them over and over and bring out new layers of meaning. She wouldn't mention God at first, because she would be unsure to whom she was talking, and she would know that the mention of God to the wrong person at an art opening can be professional suicide. Mark you as a crazy person. A contemporary artist is already suspected of that without God being involved. So Erastus would ask her very seriously if she felt God's call in this work. She would know at once that he was earnest in this question and would answer truthfully. That she is listening for God's whisperings all the time but sometimes the silence is deafening. Like Emily Dickinson, she reaches for the patterns of heaven in her art.

For a decade of my career I worked in downtown Boston on State Street, one of the earliest thoroughfares in the city that came up from Long Wharf to the Old State House. At some moment I was reading *The Miracle of Mindfulness* by Thich Nhat Hanh, a Buddhist monk. I would ride to work on the subway practicing "mindfulness" which I think of as anchoring oneself so thoroughly in the moment you are in and the place you are at that you bring yourself into a kind of perfect vibration with the universe. I would come out of the subway stop under the Old State House and a couple of times I had a distinct sensation of the spirits of other centuries in the street around me. For a fleeting moment I could actually sense the odd cut and color of a coat flashing by. The sensation was astonishing, and not, I think, entirely imagined, because it only happened two or three times, and then I lost my ability to feel it. I got too distracted.

A long life is full of surprising moments of insight, or momentary connection to something previously unsuspected. Or maybe it is an intuitive life. One year I wrote down all my dreams and got so good at it that I began to look forward to sleep like the prospect of going to the movies. I could recall on waking the most remarkable stories and places I had been to, peopled by astonishing folk. I could morph into a flying fish, or visit an Arabian souk, or a medieval town with complex water and dyke systems on a bright, windy day. I could stand with my mother on the edge of a tidal wave. It was almost unbearably rich and finally too intense to sustain. But it made me realize that we only use a tiny fraction of our brain in our waking life.

This relationship to Erastus is steadier but I know I will not always be able to feel this close to him, to call him to me in this way. Now he is so real I can see him walk the uneven pavement stones of the old city of Boston, through the Common, up Beacon Hill to the State House. Into the Parker House where he often stayed in the years he was in the State Legislature: from 1844 to 1852 and in 1857 and 1864. I can see him on the train from Springfield to Boston, reading the paper and making notes for his speeches. Conferring with colleagues. I can see him climbing onto the stagecoach in front of the general store in Northampton. In 1844 he was elected President of the

Connecticut River Railroad, created to build the next section of rail linking Northampton to Springfield. The trip to Boston in 1844 took some eight and a half hours so he stayed for days, sometimes weeks, at a time.

Peter finds my communing with the dead disquieting and tells me I need to give it up, but I point out that his love of theatre is not so far removed: he's just communing with fictional characters. At least my imagined friends were once alive.

Peter and I go to a concert at Fanueil Hall. The Boston Classical Orchestra is playing the Brahms Violin Concerto and Mendelssohn's Scotch Symphony. Neither of us has ever heard a concert in this most famous of Boston public halls. I have been here for many other kinds of public events but not a concert, and I am suspicious that this might be because the acoustics aren't right for music. We are seated towards the front of the hall in the side gallery, looking at the conductor from the vantage point of the violin section. The first notes take me by surprise. It is an exquisite sound, and the atmosphere is like an intimate small European nineteenth-century concert hall. The first movement of the "Scotch Symphony" has a grand ghostliness about it, moving from a sad lamenting minor key to a bright shaft of dancing daylight. It was as if the orchestra had summoned Erastus back to this place; I could almost see him on the stage twenty feet away from me, thundering against the proposition that Texas be permitted into the Union as a slave state. "When you are called upon," he said, "to decide what the institutions of that immense country [Texas] will be... for all time, let this be your answer: that no compromise is allowable, no compromise is possible... Freedom must and will prevail while slavery will wear away."

Mendelssohn was born a year before Erastus and a half a world away. He died at thirty-eight not long after Willie. The Scotch Symphony was published just eight years before this speech that Erastus made on this stage, and Erastus would surely have heard it and loved it. A physical place, like Faneuil Hall or the battlefield at Gettysburg, has an awesome power to forever hold the spirit of those souls whose passions were acted out in that space, and to reveal them to those who are looking and are alert to their presence.

Erastus had moved a long distance on the topic of slavery from 1834 to 1850, from being secretary of the Colonization Society to standing on the stage of Faneuil Hall as a Free Soil Party leader. I come across another snippet in the newspaper files from 1856, giving a series of quotes from eminent Americans against the extension of slavery. Erastus is sandwiched between Charles Sumner and Stephen Foster. He says: "If peaceful means fail us, and we are driven to the last extremity where ballots are useless, then we'll make bullets effective." The same quote pops up from a Southern source a few articles later. *The Macon Weekly Telegraph* writes, under the headline "Northern Fanaticism": Abolitionism has now reached its crisis. It has come to a point where it must either consume itself from its own intensity or it must involve in flames "the proud fabric of the Union." The article cites the words of a number of northern abolitionists, including the above bellicose quotation from Erastus, this time sandwiched between statements by Horace Mann and Charles Francis Adams. Erastus is getting radicalized. I cannot help but hear the echo of those times in the election we have just been through, of the deep division in the country, rooted in fear and in hatred. Would Erastus be startled that Obama is an African American? Or would he wonder why the legacy of slavery in America had persisted so long?

Obama's inauguration is now two weeks away and for vast numbers of people it is as though we are coming out of a very long, cold winter of hibernation. His approval rate is an astonishing eighty percent even though only half the country voted for him. The other half may have been queasy about an inexperienced or black president, but Americans are more truly afraid right now than most have ever been in their national life. We need hope. This good spirit cannot, of course, last. But we should not forget that it was here for a moment.

Linc is still in isolation.

IX

A Void in My Household and Heart

ERASTUS LIVED FOR THIRTY-TWO YEARS IN THE HOUSE that his father John built in 1824 on King Street in Northampton. When I drive by the address today I am stung by the ugliness of the auto repair shops and fast food restaurants that litter the landscape. But in the midst of them are a French Catholic church and its rectory, standing exactly on the site of Hopkins home. The house and grounds were sold to the Church in 1889 by the Trustees of the Hopkins estate, which was headed by Erastus's son Swinton. Sacred ground, I think to myself.

An old insurance map pictures a lot that is two hundred and seventy-five feet deep and four hundred feet wide. In the only picture I have of my great grandmother, Nettie, she sits in front of a long veranda that ran the length of much of the side of the house. There was a barn in back and like many New England small town households of the time, it was something of a farm, with a horse or two, some chickens and a dog to chase after them. The 1850 census lists eleven members of the Hopkins household, including three young women born in Ireland and a thirty-two year old William Marcy described as a laborer. Their next door neighbors, the J. D. Whitney family (who lived in a house built on the site of Jonathan Edwards' house) had fourteen under their roof and the children developed friendships that are alive in their letters for many years. Up and down the street lived the leading citizens of Northampton, including a well-documented agent of the Underground Railroad, J. P. Williston.

Like special people, houses can have charisma. They can spear your heart with a shaft of light, let you hear the echo of a beloved footstep coming down the stairs. Like you, they get old but they endure. They carry the spirit of the people who have lived in them. The family letters, written from that house on King Street, create a picture in my mind. I can see the room where Willie's little coffin lay under a glass cover. The room is grey-blue with white trim, about 12x16 feet, facing north. The coffin is sitting on a bench in the corner, standing out at an angle by the fireplace. Beyond is a wall of windows, looking out on a broad veranda that runs along the side of the house.

I dream often of the house we moved into when my father remarried and we suddenly were a family of eight. It was unfashionably large for the tastes of 1955, with eleven bedrooms and seven baths. Its spaces are like corners of myself that I come across with surprise. They appear to me in my dream state complete with their claw-footed furnishings that Betty would buy in auction houses. Once in a dream I raced from room to room in that big old house, discovering empty spaces on every wall where mirrors had been removed. In the last room sat Betty, on a kind of throne like the Wizard of Oz. I shouted up at her to put them back, to restore my identity. My fury woke me up.

Peter and I have lived in another house with charisma for twenty-five years, longer than either of us have ever lived anywhere before. Though smaller than the house of my dream, it might have been designed by the same architect, so alike is it in style. Now it is full of the spirit of my children and grandchildren, of Thanksgivings and music. We have had our bad moments in it too, one of them memorialized by a door panel that has a crack in it from a good swift kick I gave it the week we moved in together. I don't remember now what my momentary outburst was about, but being in a relationship involves endless transactions. Learning to submit gracefully when you've just lost an argument seems to be a never-ending process. Somehow, I can't imagine either Erastus or Charlotte kicking a door panel.

I begin to encounter evidence that some forty years after his death Erastus had become something of a hero in the folklore of Northampton—though this little flame of remembrance will be extinguished for the next hundred years or so. In an article in *New England Magazine* of 1900 I find the following reference to Erastus's home on King Street: "On one occasion a fugitive slave was hidden in the attic over the Sabbath. The children of the family visited him and told the story of Christ. His eyes glistened, and he eagerly absorbed the story, to him absolutely new. He asked the children, "Was he nailed to the cross and died for me? I would be hanged myself before I would do that." I can certainly imagine Sallie, Caro and Nettie, well trained as they were by their father, proselytizing a poor fugitive in the attic.

Hiding fugitive slaves in need would probably have been a moral imperative to Erastus. At least one of his neighbors and close friends was very active in the Underground Railroad; as president of the real railroad Erastus may have been in a position to move fugitives swiftly on the actual rails. Scouring the Underground Railroad tales of western Massachusetts, most of which were compiled by Wilbur Siebert at the end of the nineteenth century, I have found no other references to Erastus's

Underground Railroad activity. What was fact and what was fiction relating to the Underground Railroad is murky. Hiding fugitives was an illegal activity, recounted long after the fact with much fable woven in. I want it to be true, just like I wanted him to be the handsome man in the picture, but where is the hard evidence?

Almost everything I have found to piece together Erastus's life and heart are from his own words, his letters and his speeches. Primary sources. If someone were to dig around the public record for my life in two hundred years they would probably rely on an old Google archive where some bubbles of information would be blown up like great balloons, but the arc of the life and the color and flavor would be gone, like dust on the wind.

In Erastus's letters we have the private man recorded in his own voice. In his speeches we have the public man and can see his stand on the expansion of slavery, the treatment of the mentally ill, and the rise of Catholicism in Massachusetts.

In 1848 Erastus breaks from the dominant Whig party in a dramatic move and is elected by Northampton as a Free Soiler, the group that was determined to keep slavery out of the new territories. He incurs the wrath of his former colleagues and essentially ends the trajectory of his rise to power. Perhaps it is a little of that defiance that I am seeing in the photograph. He was on the path to be governor and he became instead a "Conscience Whig," vehemently arguing against the extension of slavery in the new territories and "laboring only for the advancement of a great principle." S.E. Bridgeman says, "He cast his lot in with the lowly and despised," meaning that his powerful friends did not stand by him in this moment.

Later in his life Erastus would be a delegate to the National Republican Convention that will, very unexpectedly, nominate Abraham Lincoln as their candidate for President. He knows several of the candidates personally, including Salmon P. Chase who went to Dartmouth a few years ahead of him. Like Erastus, Chase was a founder of the Free Soil Party.

While at the convention, Erastus wrote a poignant letter to him from the Freemont House in Chicago.

Fremont House, Gage, Bro. & Drake Proprietors
Chicago, May 17, 1860

My Dear Sir,

Your favor by Mr. Rice is just rec'd. Thank you for your confidence. I wish your name stood more prominent here. There are lots of good feelings afloat here for you, but there is no set of men in earnest for you. The lukewarmness of those who should not be lukewarm is your misfortune. The Ohio Delegation does not seem to be any where as yet.

I think the hardest kind of death to die is that occasioned by indecisive, or lukewarm friends.

New York is in earnest.

In haste,
Yours truly
Erastus Hopkins

Faithful are the words of a friend—is the expression of my apology to you. I am your friend.

The tone is a curious combination of very respectful and very frank, as would befit a celebrated member of an earlier class at Dartmouth, perhaps a college friend of his brother's. Chase was a man whose radical abolitionist stance in the 1850s and 60s matched Erastus's almost exactly, who had undergone a religious conversion, and who was afflicted with a level of hubris that dogs his reputation to the present day. But I also read in this letter the sadness of a man who has been disappointed in his friends at times, and does not want to be such a friend to Chase.

But let's go back to the year 1849 because it's a defining moment in America, and for Erastus too. It was the year that gold was discovered in California, and people of every color and stripe rushed to that once sleepy village of Buena Vista. They created in almost a single moment the city of San Francisco, a wild and greedy place, and in its single mindedness, oddly tolerant of all those different kinds of people. They were mostly men, so they mostly ate out, leaving that city today with some of the best restaurants in the country and an unmatched food culture. Boston, in the same moment, was dealing with floods of Irish immigrants fleeing from the potato famine, too poor for passage beyond the wharves they were deposited on (the height of the famine was 1848 to 1852). In three decades Boston's population tripled, overwhelming the small, closely knit Anglo-American population that had had virtually no disruption in its social fabric for two hundred years. No impetus for a restaurant culture here: Boston's native population turned inward, to their private clubs and domestic dining tables, now staffed by Irish serving girls. And the Irish turned their bitter disdain, well earned by the British for their part in turning a famine into a genocide, on the Brahmin class of Bostonians.

I am roiled with anxiety about my white Anglo-Saxon protestant heritage. We weren't nice to those Irish immigrants. There is no denying it. Along with his anti-slavery activities, Erastus, as a state legislator, was right in the middle of the political action that stemmed from this sudden new population. He was on the committee that declared public education to be compulsory in 1852. And in 1849 he was vocal in opposing the granting of a charter to Jesuits for the College of the Holy Cross College in Worcester.

Holy Cross had been founded six years before, but its diplomas were being signed in the name of the College of Maryland (Loyola). Every educational institution in Massachusetts, then and now, operates under a charter granted by the state that spells out its responsibilities as an institution serving the public. Erastus's published speeches on the subject are easy to find and I hold them in my hand with trepidation. One of them says: "Before granting the prayer of the petitioners we ought, perhaps, to consider whether it is expedient to sanction a system of education which commits the entire training of youth, from the tender age of 8 years and even less, to Celibates,—men who, by their strongest religious views and vows, have separated themselves from all the refining and beneficial influences of social life." He argues that the charter seekers are not asking for equal privileges, but special privileges because they are seeking to create a college to which non-Catholics would be denied entry, the only such institution in the country. "We cannot legislate for a class, or sect, distinct from the community...We have common laws, common institutions, common schools, common colleges—a general community of interests—what one may enjoy all may enjoy—we have, in all these schools, colleges, institutions, and laws, an ancient and glorious *Common-wealth*...."

Reading Erastus's arguments against granting the Jesuits a charter, I see a man of supreme rationality who musters argument after argument around precedents for exclusive educational institutions, separation of church and state, the Common-wealth and the liberty of American society. But his heart is truly revealed when he says: "The great and distinctive feature of the Roman Catholic system is, *that they interpose an Hierarchy and a Priesthood between men's souls and their* God... Kings and Emperors, even, sued for temporal and eternal salvation, at the gates of Rome... It was not till Luther arose, and, sweeping away these Hierarchs and Priests, took the poor peasantry by the hand, and taught them the glorious truth, that they could go directly to God and, all alone, far away from priests and altar, in the retirement of their cabins, where no eye could see them but the eye of God, and no ear could hear them but the ear of God,—pour out the tears of deep contrition, and utter the voice of complaint and supplication before Him..." In that paragraph lie hundreds of years of tortured misery between Catholics and Protestants. It's a misery

I have always thought of as a piece of history, but see now as having something of a continuing life and unspoken presence in Massachusetts and particularly Boston, where a political culture of petty revenge has been diligently nurtured. The Holy Cross charter was finally granted in the 1860s, some fifteen years later, but this fiercely polite standoff was characteristic of the relationship between the two major religious groups in the Commonwealth.

In 1852 the newspapers are full of Erastus and Lajos Kossuth, Hungarian martyr, hero, soldier, poet, a man fighting for Hungarian independence and identity in the European revolutionary fervor that ignited in 1848. He is touring America to gain support for the Hungarian cause and Erastus brings him to Massachusetts, and home to Sunday dinner. Thousands turn out to hear him speak. The Kossuth tour awakened an unembarrassed patriotic pride for Americans in their beautiful country and its freedoms. He was like they imagined their grandpas, a freedom fighter, a man of great principle. He connected them to an older, proud national narrative at a moment when all seemed close to collapse from the divisions around slavery. I felt that same surge of national pride in the early days of the Obama presidency, in my daughter's lament that this was the first moment of her life that she had been proud of her country.

After the 2008 election, Doris Kearns Goodwin's *Team of Rivals*, about Lincoln's cabinet, was being daily cited in the newspapers, as Obama started to put together his own cabinet, picking his arch-rival, Hillary Clinton, for Secretary of State first. The Presidential election of 2008 which riveted the nation for almost two years was eerily resonant of the 1860 election that brought Lincoln to the Presidency. The country was locked into bitter and opposing camps and nothing was too scurrilous to be said of the other.

I come home one day and find a letter from Linc. Four handwritten pages on lined paper. He has been moved to the Middlesex

County Jail in Cambridge. He starts off: "Thank you so much for the wonderful letter I found some interesting insights in it. Especially the information on Erastus Hopkins." He has paid close attention. On the envelope he includes his middle name, Sewall, which was my grandmother's maiden name and his grandfather's first name. Linc is a descendent of the first chief justice of Massachusetts.

He writes a kind of stream of consciousness that feels like a drowning person reaching for another's hand. No breath drawn. He is happy to have been moved from Billerica House of Corrections where he was in "segregation." No radio, no canteen and no basketball. Now in Cambridge he has these and life is better. He's struggling with his medications. They make him fuzzy and sleepy. He used to sleep only four or five hours but now he's in bed for eight or nine. His mother keeps him supplied with books and he loves Ken Follett and Jack London. I suspect that she also picks his magazines which include *National Geographic*, *Rolling Stone*, *Sports Illustrated* and *Men's Health*. He describes his sisters' visit with their two little one-year-old girls and speculates that he will not see his nieces again until they are about five. They blew him kisses as they left. He wrote to thank his sisters for visiting. My image of this scene comes straight out of a movie. I will keep writing.

In the 1850s Dorothea Dix convinced the Massachusetts State Legislature to fund the creation of a new breed of humane mental hospitals. Her passion for improving the plight of the mentally ill stemmed from a visit to the East Cambridge Jail in 1841, where she found the inmates in appalling conditions. She visited the location, though I trust not the same building, from which Linc wrote his letter. Following Dix's arguments, Erastus persuaded the legislature to locate a state "lunatic asylum" in Northampton. His argument for the healthful qualities of Northampton resulted in the construction of a 250 bed Kirkebride hospital that opened in 1856. It was a model institution when it began but over the next hundred and forty years, it grew like a series of rabbit warrens and in the mid-1950s housed as many as 2500 patients. The humane impulse of the original hospital was gradually forgotten, and for years the Northampton State Hospital, as it came to be called, was simply a warehouse for the mentally ill; treatments were scant. Schizophrenia was not recognized as a disease until the late nineteenth century and pharmacological treatments didn't begin until the 1950s. Treatment today is extraordinary by comparison, but many, like Linc, are not recognized as ill until they are in trouble with the law, sometimes big trouble.

I read his letter several times and that night I dream of his family. In the dream they live in an historic house and had small ponies that all the children rode, except Linc who was kept in a kind of animal pen. The setting was pastoral, Northampton-like. His mother, very dear to me, was so sad. I woke up in the night in a sweat, thinking of Linc's isolation. The leaden weight of this particular family pain has taken six years to settle itself in my heart.

* * *

In 1864 Caro, at eighteen, is suddenly taken with dysentery in the summer. She dies in a few short days. I look at the register of births and deaths in the Northampton Town Hall and see that others die in this summer from the same thing. Perhaps the water supply was polluted. Today this would be a wholly preventable death. For Erastus this is the sixth of his children to die and for Charlotte the fifth. The Civil War hangs like the sword of Damocles over Swinton who is serving in the Union Army in Louisiana. Nettie, from boarding school, writes anguished letters questioning her father's God.

Shortly after Caro's death, Erastus writes to Nettie of a comforting visit from Ned and Alice Whitney, the children of their neighbors. I am taken back to a moment many years ago when I was a senior in college and my stepbrother, Mat, was killed in a car accident. Mat whom we had dropped off at boarding school on that weekend of my father and stepmother's

Lake Placid honeymoon twelve years earlier. We were almost the same age. He was at the University of Colorado and I was at Brown. The police in Boulder relayed the news to the Brookline police. A uniformed officer rang the bell of our front door in the middle of the night to tell my parents. The family gathered from all corners of the country and helplessly watched his mother Betty's paroxysms of grief. Each of us was strangely isolated in our own bubble of incomprehension and sadness. His short life had been very hard, with many eye surgeries, his father's death in an airplane crash, boarding school at eight years old and the outsized dramas of our merged family. His death held the trauma of a suicide though it was not; we could hardly speak of it. I remember someone saying to me at the time: "Every life is a complete life, whether it's long or short." It was the only comfort I could think to take...the faintest wisp of faith. Reading of the young Whitneys coming to call on Erastus and Charlotte after Caro's death brought back a memory of my college roommates and their boyfriends cooking a special meal for my parents in the gothic dining room of 87 Prospect Street, our elegant dorm at Brown. They served my parents lobster and made a tight circle of sympathy and youthful hope in the midst of their terrible grief. Later Erastus writes this letter to Nettie.

October 15 1865 Northampton, Sabbath PM

My Dear Darling Daughter,

A void in my household & heart has made me ask today "Where's Nettie?" The answer came provokingly back "Upstairs." Well so you may be, but up stairs to which I cannot travel; & there in that attic, is the young heart brimming over with bright and sparkling love and I cannot touch the material form which is quickened into life by its warm pulsations. But though my voice said no more, my soul followed up the inquiry "Where's Nettie?" with "Where's Caro? And Lottie and Johnnie and Willie?" Sweet ones! They are where we must soon go. It seems as if all the lovely spirits of earth were being garnered in the skies, and our beautiful places are left desolate. This house once so full of life & joy is large, lonesome, dreary. Your absence, my loved one, contributes much to this feeling. I am sad in my own home. I ache in my own nest. The nooks and the corners, in doors and out of doors, once so full of blithe and happy hearts are now only suggestions of desolation.

I never knew favorites among my children, but, somehow Caro was always dear to me. As a little child, though always sweet, she had less of personal & demonstrative attractiveness than her sisters, & this led me always to feel jealous lest she should be understated, & hence, I suppose, my heart was drawn forth more tenderly toward her. I think I more early & readily recognized the years of her preeminent goodness than did others, & was accustomed to "stand up" for her & insist upon her bright promise... And then such a sweet, calm, perfect, instructive, soothing sunset to her life, as she dropped from the zenith to her eternal rest. Who ever anticipated that? Who ever, without vision could conceive such an end to life.

My darling, sainted child! How often you are with my thoughts, & how often, by day and by night, the sweet, but still aching memories of you, prompt my sighs, no one can know.

But I would not recall her! No, dear me, thou hast attained that eternal life which I always covet as the highest boon for my children, thy warfare's o'er-thy victory's won. Little did I think that the ripening of thine earthly youthful life was to pass literally into the angelic. The beautiful earthly type passed into the heavenly reality.

I ought not, perhaps, so to write—a father to a youngest child. But I want to tell somebody & I ask leave to pour my parents thoughts into your child bosom.

And bless you dearest, & may angels watch over you here, & receive you hereafter—God will determine how soon—we have nothing to do about it–sure to rejoice in His will. It is a joy to have you here. It is a joy to have Caro & the little band in heaven.

> *Your affectionate Father*

He sits alone at home thinking of all his children, and whether they are at school or in heaven they are both vividly present and sadly absent. *Up stairs to which I cannot travel...* When I first read this letter it seems to me to have a touch of madness in it. At the time I, too, am sitting alone at home and this spirit voice of Erastus the angel, whispering loudly in my ear of the power of faith and the power of family. He is my best companion.

Four years later, I am surrounded by family. I have been re-discovered. My daughter, Jody, and her husband now have two children under three and have moved from New York to be five minutes from her mother's rescuing care. Hannah lives five minutes in the other direction and invites me regularly to join her in the local hot tub. My husband, Peter, has moved home and we take care of our grandchildren two days a week. I watch him, a man who has twice married women with cute five year olds but never had his "own" children, climbing under the piano to play hide and seek with two-year-old Eamon. I am amazed at this new side of him. We are suddenly plunged into a new unforeseen stage of life.

Little Sadie, Swint's daughter, glows like a bright beam in Erastus's life and I am totally with him. He writes her this little note when she is seven:

Ocean House, Cape Elizabeth Maine, Saturday, July 27, 1867
My Dear Sadie,

If there was a window in my heart, & you could look right in, what do you think you would see there, just at this moment? I can tell you, you would see a little girl of seven years with white hair combed straight back, with a round comb on over the top of her head, listening to her papa as he reads a letter to her. She has

*blue eyes & is tall and bony & finds it hard work to sit or stand
still. You would see her sometimes on a hard bench at school,
studying her lesson & looking occasionally around the room
at those little boys, then saying her lesson to the teacher. After
school you would see her trotting down stairs and playing—then
sitting in her mama's room with a little young man in her lap
smiling and looking at her. All this is in my heart, and I want to
shut up the window so that nobody can see in & and I can have
a good time with my Sadie.*

    Your loving Dante

For his grandchildren Erastus had taken on the nickname
Dante and communicated his love and faith as actively as he did
with his own children. Charlotte was Mamama. Peter and I are
Babbo and Oma.

X

The Wolf at the Door: War and Homesickness

I HAVE NOW SPENT MANY HOURS IN HISTORICAL ARCHIVES in three states combing through files looking for the handwriting of the favorite members of my family. The work is solitary and intimate. I am peeling back layers of reality and time, bringing this gentle chatter back to life. I am not present in their world, I am held in some suspended future that they cannot yet imagine. And they might easily not have been in mine, but here they are, lifting my spirits like real friends do.

I am learning to be more organized but I realize I do not have the objective and meticulous character of a true historian. I copy and transcribe each letter and put it into chronological sequence, so that no matter which archive they came from, they come together like the pieces of a puzzle. Sometimes I get a clear picture of what's happening, and sometimes the letters just stop. They are all at home and shut me out.

I am beginning to see patterns and personalities emerging. Mary Annette, known as Nettie, coming into adolescence, is a spark plug in the family, maybe even in the town. She's a teenager, a little drunk with life. She flicks her red hair as she passes her neighbor and would be boy friend, Ned Whitney, on the street. In one letter she says "when I see any very handsome students generally the temptation is too great and before I know it I am flirting with them." She has a "new black bonnet trimmed with scarlet and gold and another English hat turned up straight all around

trimmed with black plumes and velvet." Ah, she is vain. I am
watching my granddaughter Margaret, almost two, discovering
her own powers, as she lowers her chin and looks up at us with
her devilish smile, holding the forbidden marbles in her hand
before us, testing our reaction to her big blue eyes. I give her a
new red coat with a plaid lining and she won't take it off for days.
She is not shy, not cautious like her brother. She is forthright and
determined and athletic. I see this personality in her fourth great
grandmother, Nettie.

In a letter in 1861 to her friend Lammie, fourteen-year-old
Nettie describes her "gay little Louane Company consisting of
about a dozen girls of my size and smaller. The officers are Capt.
Nettie Hopkins, ahem! 1st Lt Edith Eddy; 2nd Lt Nellie Cook.
Orderly sergeant, Hattie Parsons." Then she describes an elabo-
rate uniform with "Red Louane" pants, dark blue shirts trimmed
with white and red turban caps which she has carefully drawn, as
well as a blue "Garibaldi" jacket. "Our weapons are poles about
six feet in length painted red white and blue with a ball on both
ends." They drilled on Saturday mornings on the Northampton Common where they must have created quite a stir in the
town. The letter is charmingly illustrated with little inky soldiers
looking like medieval Italians and speaking commands in big

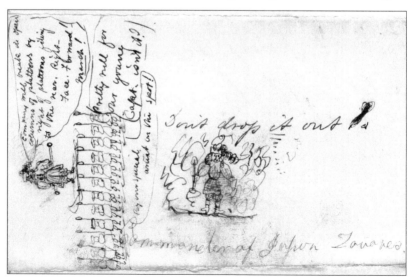

balloons. They even have a Constitution that includes things like Rule 3: No laughing, talking, or disorder in the ranks.

At the moment she is writing this, her adored twenty-six-year-old brother Swinton is a lieutenant in the Massachusetts Thirty-First Regiment and stationed in a very uncomfortable barracks at Camp Seward in Pittsfield. Possibly this spirited girl is just a little more than her parents feel that they can manage at home, for she is now sent off to Lawrence Academy in Groton under great protest, signing herself Capt. Nettie in her letters home to her friends. Her more obedient and demure older sister Caro goes with her and together they spend the next several years as boarders. Some of Erastus's most beautiful letters come from this period of separation from his daughters.

The Civil War had begun in earnest with the attack on Fort Sumter in April of 1861. Swinton had signed up that fall, leaving his wife Lizzie and year-and-a-half baby Sadie in Ware, where he had just established himself as a young lawyer. Much concern now swirls around this little family. But Nettie and Caro off in boarding school get regular letters from their father and their mother, transmitting news of Swinton and Lizzie and lots of sweetly delivered moral instruction.

On December 29, 1861 Erastus wrote separate letters to both girls that give some flavor of his feeling for each of them and how different they probably were. The first to Nettie:

Northampton December 29 1861

My Dear Darling Goslin—My overgrown Baby

My Dear Nettie,

Your part of "Friday Morn's" letter addressed to me was very welcome. You think of me then? & that it is "too bad" that I am so little thought of & so much neglected. And your little heart sent forth its quaking tribute of affection. Thank you, sweet one, for the dry sod of our old hearts is made as glad by the smiles and caresses of the young, as is the arid earth by a summer shower.

*And the buds & blossoms & fruits of a tender affection have
already put forth and ripened and I send the rich trophies of your
girlish husbandry back to you; to wit, a father's love, a father's
kisses and a father's caresses. May you ever keep these emotions
young and fresh within me. I will give you the treasures of
my wisdom, counsel & care in exchange for your artless and
pure affections & thus we will try to drive a brisk & mutually
enriching commerce while life lasts.*

*You must quicken up that tardy watch of yours which cheats
you out of an hour of precious morning time.*

*I am very glad to hear that you like your school "very much
indeed." But you proceed to say that there are only two girls
whom you like, but the boys are all stealing locks of your hair
& secreting them in their watch cases! Is that why you like the
school? Fie! That you should be so captivated by Barber-ous boys!
I hope you will not degenerate into the barbarous life!*

*But, to be sober, I suppose that you intended what you said—
that you liked the school. No intelligence could give me greater
pleasure. For I am quite sure that Uncle Charles will so conduct
his school that it will not be liked "very much indeed" by those
who are not reasonably fond of study...*

Your affectionate father, Gander

They have a bantering, playful relationship, these two. She
quickens his heart and he feels her adolescent energy and excitement with life. I was a teenager like this, always on the brink of
something my parents would not approve of, often over the
brink. Like stealing a bottle of wine from the cellar to ride around
with my friends, or sneaking into my boyfriend's Harvard dorm
room. My father was quite oblivious unless he happened to catch
me red-handed, which on occasion he did. But he was not given
to articulating his moral point of view on the world. Maybe that
habit died with the decline of letter writing.

Charlotte writes Nettie too.

...And now Pussy, I have been afraid from what I have seen
of you at home, that you might be a little too familiar with the
young gentlemen—and I want to guard you particularly about
that-I hope the young men there are good young men, who do
nothing wrong, but when you write about them cutting off your
hair, I am afraid that you were allowing them to be too familiar.
    Supposing that they should cut off Caro's hair. Can you
suppose such a thing? Now I want you to have some of Caro's
dignity of character.

Later in this same letter she cautions her on negative gossiping:

    ...You must see the good that is in her. And overlook what
does not suit your fancy. And by no means allow yourself to talk
about her, because that will only strengthen any prejudices that
you have."

Reading these letters so full of moral instruction makes me
ponder the ways in which I have imparted such messages to my
children. Rather haphazardly, I fear.

To Caroline Erastus writes:

Northampton, December 29th, 1861

My Dear Caro,
    I resume an old habit of writing to you. Well do I remember
the gusto with which I used to seat myself, in the far of western
land, to write to a quiet little girl of your name, whose life has
been absorbed into that of the majestic lady whom I have the
honor to address. I love to remember how tenderly my heart was
accustomed to go forth toward you, & how I associated you with
every pleasing thing, or with every thing which I thought might
be pleasing to your infant eyes-even down to the glittering foil
which encased John Anderson's "Solace." And you are not the only

one I then loved. There were others the remembrance of whom
used to make my heart verdant & young. Two of them are still
amidst the trials of earth, with their feet amid the thorny path of
life, & two are in heaven where there are not thorns & thistles.
I have no care now for the latter, while my care and anxieties
for the former are constantly increasing. Life still stretches out
before you, & who knows what it contains. The troubles now
in our land, so sudden & so severe show the wickedness of earth
& how uncertain are all our treasures, even our property & our
most sweet endearments of home. If you are safe in heaven, I
should have no such cares concerning you & now I care only that
you may walk bravely, patiently & honorably the road which lies
longer & more wearily before you, than the short and lithesome
one which Lottie & Johnnie traveled.

These are some of the thoughts and feelings which your
father has toward his children. And now let me ask you to devote
yourself with all diligence to that preparation for usefulness &
happiness in life for which you are sent to school. Be studious &
make steady progress. Form good & regular habits, & above all
cultivate a spirit of conscientiousness and true piety. When Paul's
eyes were opened, he asked but one question "Lord what will
thou have me to do?" Seek to guide every hour of your life by this
spirit & be happy in doing just what is right & true.

> *Farewell sweet Caro,*
> *Your Father*

Charlotte writes this postscript:

My dear Chick, …. Tell Nettie she must not be too friendly with
this young gentleman. Does she go over to the Academy alone
in the eveng to practice? I do not quite like to have her. A very
Happy New Year to you all–Farewell. Very affectionately Mama

There's an eerie quality to this letter from Erastus to Caro, as if he anticipates that she will be soon "safe in heaven."

I go searching in the Gutman Education Library at Harvard and find a history of Lawrence Academy. The Preceptor, or Head of the school, from 1853 to 1863 was Charles Hammond. Charlotte had a younger sister, Adrianna, and I deduce that this may be Aunt Addie, married to Charles Hammond, and that the girls are boarding in their home. Nonetheless, Nettie's interest in boys seems to have her mother a little concerned.

The domestic past of my imagination is oddly sanitized, days are sunny, people always in good cheer and great grandmothers are dressed in corsets and hoops, prim and impenetrable. But people, being what they are, in full bloom at sixteen or so, Nettie may have done quite a bit of experimenting. She was that kind of girl.

On the whole, Erastus's letters to Nettie are more playful, sometimes more sermonic, as if he is responding to her lively, daring spirit. His letters to Caro are gentle, almost wistful—full of advice, but with an underlying feeling that it is hardly needed. Caro is the almost too good child. No one saved her letters. My theory is that Nettie was the saver, and since they were always together, Caro never wrote to her, so she had nothing to save. A friend of Nettie's offered this little glimpse of Caro in a later letter: "Do you not remember how eagerly she watched for every paper: how beyond every girl in school she was always posted in all that pertained to our army and their movements—How her eyes would glisten and her cheeks flush as she busily read the long columns!" By the end of 1862 the two girls are at the Ipswich Female Seminary on the North Shore in Massachusetts. I dare speculate that all those boys proved to be too worrisome a proposition for the parents.

With a brother writing regularly from "the front," the girls were following the war with a very personal concentration. Looking now at the nightly television news bringing bloody skir-

mishes and terrorist attacks into our living rooms from around
the world, I think how inured we have become in our modern
world to violence. How might the Civil War have been different
if they had seen it on television every day? Would it have been
intolerable to see Americans killing each other with such fury, or
would they have become numb as we have?

July of 1863 was meltingly hot in Louisiana, heavy with hu-
midity and infested with mosquitoes. In one letter Swinton illus-
trates his heat rash with tiny dots all over a penned figure. In the
critical first week of July 1863 he wrote to Nettie:

> *Head Quarters 31st Mass Vols [volunteers], Beaufort,*
> *Port Hudson La July 6. 1863*
>
> *My dear Nettie,*
> *A mail a day or two since brought me two nice long letters*
> *from Caro & yourself and as I wrote her last, I shall answer*
> *yours this time. Here we sit still making very slow advances*
> *yet I hope sure ones on this great stronghold of the Mississippi*
> *River. For nearly seven weeks now we have lived in this great*
> *Magnolia Forest with constant firing going on, sometimes light*
> *& sometimes heavy, as the opportunity of observation on the*
> *enemy's movements (or theirs on ours). We have had two regular*
> *and bloody assaults, May 27th and June 14th and since the last*
> *of these we have been digging. I think had we taken to the spade*
> *at first, we should have been in Port Hudson by this time, but*
> *I don't know as General Banks is to be blamed for not knowing*
> *what he was to find here. No reliable information could ever be*
> *gained about this ravined place.*
>
> *You can have no idea of the extent of its natural defences. We*
> *have fought our way in… through the forest passing ravine after*
> *ravine of great depth…full of vines and tangled underbrush,*
> *more numerous and presenting a wilder sight than anything*
> *you can find about home…The forest here is full of insects and*
> *creeping things. My special abhorrence of snakes has given me*

but little trouble in Louisiana except in imagination and dread. I have not heard of a case of injury from reptiles in our whole march of 300 miles and our whole stay here. We came here May 23rd making this the forty-sixth day of the siege, and we are getting very tired of it I assure you.

Your account of your daily routine of duty as we call it in the army, makes quite a favorable impression of your school on me. You seem to be busy and I tell you that is everything in the world. Every day of my life shows more and more plainly to use the truth of the old saw about Satan & idle hands. You see this nothing to do is what an army conducting a siege (is about)... The lazy hours of this siege have made us all most miserable in body & mind...[the letter continues] *July 8th, 1863. Yesterday the glorious news of the surrender of Vicksburg reached us and while I write our Generals are arranging the surrender of Port Hudson...this is considered a virtual surrender for no terms will be granted unless a mere courtesy of some kind to the officers who have conducted so full out a defence. General Gardner, of course, well knows it. We are just about ready for a renewed and decisive attack but I think the blood will be saved before night.*

I think I may be the first to inform you that the Mississippi is open from source to mouth. The greatest achievement of the war!

Ever affly Your Brother
WSBHopkins

This letter is written three days after the Battle of Gettysburg had finally turned the tide of the war in favor of the Union Army. In its wake, Vicksburg, the last confederate stronghold on the Mississippi, surrendered after a six-week siege, effectively cutting the Confederacy in two and separating it from its western alliances. The toll of American lives was staggering at that point and the war would continue for almost two more years, until Lee's surrender on April 9, 1865. In the end nearly three-quarters of-a-million men died in battle or of battle related injuries, and hundreds of thousands were horribly wounded. To put that in context, in 1860 the entire population, free and slave, was thirty-one-and-a-half million.

Six days after Swinton's letter, New York City was into the second day of the first American draft. The names of all those eligible to be drafted were contained in an iron drum from which they were to be drawn until the quota was reached. A furious firestorm against the draft had been whipped up by the press and fed by the Governor's insistence that it overstepped Federal prerogatives. The building was stormed by some five hundred stone-and-bat wielding laborers, triggering a riot that went unchecked for five days and terrorized the city. Blacks were pursued and beaten to death wherever they were spotted, and their bodies hung from trees. In all, more than a thousand people were killed or injured.

As all of this is happening a soldier in the Lincoln Hospital in Washington writes to the girls, who clearly have been doing their own war duty.

Lincoln Hospital, Ward 6, Washington DC July 3, 1863

Dear unknown friend,

Your comfort bag as you call it—containing so many little valuables was handed to me yesterday by a friend with a request that I should send you a few lines acknowledging the receipt of the same—But dear friend be assured that your trouble was not in vain—if you are a true friend of your countries defenders— for the contents did cheer and animate my spirits very much and the little gifts you conferred upon me did make at least one happy moment in my soldier life....Oh how I wish that this desperate war was over—and we could all return to our loved ones at home—now dear unknown friend I must bid you adieu by imploring you to be forever true to the union and its defenders— From your country's friend—

Henry Wheat
Co 64th Reg—NY

Despite, or perhaps because of, the elegant handwriting, I suspect this letter (much longer than what is printed here) is not entirely genuine—that it was a form that was copied by many, full of appropriate wartime sentiments, but without a shred of detail of the sender's life. Perhaps a fleet of volunteers penned these thoughts in response to all the items pouring in from around the country. Walt Whitman, who sometimes worked as a nurse in Union hospitals said "Future years, will never know the seething hell, the black infernal background of the minor scenes and interiors...of the Secession War, and it is best they should not." Some of those scenes were happening at the Lincoln Hospital. It had been created, almost overnight in 1862 on Capitol Hill, one of many temporary hospitals erected in the Civil War. To a bird flying it would have looked like a flock of geese in their usual V formation, the V, in this case, being made up of a series of long tents that could house more than 2200 wounded soldiers. Few of them were probably up to the task of writing elegant letters of thanks. But I have no doubt that receiving Henry Wheat's missive thrilled Nettie and Caro, and that it was passed around and read aloud to the class.

About the time I encounter these particular letters, I go to a dance performance of Bill T. Jones/Arnie Zane Dance Company that is oddly titled *Another Evening: Serenade/The Proposition*. The piece is raw and chaotic. Primed by these letters, I am transported like a shocked recruit into the black hole of war. Strange repetitive movement sequences, stentorian repetition of phrases from Lincoln's speeches, and the searing words of the "Battle Hymn of the Republic" pull me into their maelstrom, their endless swirling daguerreotype tableaus. A group of women in dignified poses, spins into a physical sequence of pulling together and apart, of conflict and cooperation. A woman standing between two fighting men cries "It's hard to ride two horses at once." Behind them are giant black and white projections of the dead and the barely living and of their cities burned: Richmond, Atlanta, Charleston,

Gettysburg, Vicksburg. The recitation of the words of Julia Ward Howe's "Battle Hymn of the Republic" are, just plainly spoken without music, searing. *Mine eyes have seen the glory of the coming of the Lord: He is trampling out the vintage where the grapes of wrath are stored; He hath loosed the fateful lightening of his terrible swift sword; His truth is marching on. I have seen him in the watch fires of a hundred circling camps; They have builded him an altar in the evening dews and damps...He is sifting out the hearts of men before His judgment seat...In the beauty of the lilies he was born across the sea, with a glory in His bosom that transfigures you and me: As he died to make men holy, let us die to make men free....*

The piece knocks the breath out of me. I feel blood rush to my brain, and oddly, I salivate. Literally, the piece makes me drool. My body is overtaken, transcended. Jones is searching for the context of his own history here. It ends with his mental parallel between Lincoln entering Richmond at the end of the war, and his own family arriving there on a trip in his childhood. In puzzling over that connection, I suddenly think of that moment in my life when I retrieved my mother's medical records from forty years before. The evening of the day I had spent reading them I was at a tribute dinner to the victims of McCarthyism. I had a realization that stunned me for a moment: my mother had had her mastectomy in the first week of the McCarthy Hearings. It anchored her pain very specifically for me. The confluence of very personal history and huge national drama magnifies the poignancy and pain of both events. The big and the small become intertwined and concrete. Bill T. Jones is reconquering Richmond for himself.

He comes out at the end of the evening and gives us the black power salute, a gesture I haven't seen in many years. It is the month before Barack Obama will be elected President. It is a month in which we are wondering where the bottom of the stock market might be. The terrible swift sword is visible in our midst.

The "Battle Hymn of the Republic" is an American abolitionist song. Julia Ward Howe wrote the lyrics in November of 1861 and they were published in the Atlantic Monthly in February of

1862. In all likelihood the Hopkins family knew Julia Ward Howe and were subscribers to the Atlantic. I imagine their household ringing with the Hymn and that they were deeply stirred by it in the context of the war and their own spiritual roots.

Julia Ward Howe would have been nine years younger than Erastus. The Howes traveled to Rome on their honeymoon (as Erastus and Charlotte had two years earlier) in the company of Horace and Jane Mann and traveled in Europe with Charles Sumner. Erastus sent Nettie Charles Sumner's autograph in 1861. Newspaper records often talk of Hopkins, Mann and Sumner in the same columns and they shared abolitionist speaking platforms in the 1840s and 1850s. These highly educated descendents of the early Calvinists travelled in the same paths and shared a deeply held set of values. One can only speculate on exactly whom Erastus knew and liked, but Julia Ward Howe is a pretty likely bet.

Long after I have stopped searching the archives for new traces of Erastus, a letter comes to me by email from someone who is doing an exhibit on the Underground Railroad in Vermont. It is the indisputable evidence I have been searching for that Erastus was an agent of the UGRR, aiding fugitive slaves on their route to Canada. It also makes clear that he is no stranger to *Uncle Tom's Cabin*. It is addressed to his nephew, the son of his sister who was married to the president of the University of Vermont.

Northampton July 11th 1859
John B. Wheeler Esq.

Believe the heavens & do that which is right.

My Dear Nephew,

For the first-time I act as Prest of the Underground Railroad, having abjured all connection with those that use above ground. I have given Bill a note to you which he will present in person. He is directed to a Mr. William French in your town. His story is true, beyond a question.

He wants to go to Chatham in Canada West, near Detroit.
Had probably better go by Ogdensburg, & thence by steamer to
Lewiston, thence by railroad. Rouse's Point is a place where he
may be watched.

He is the son of his Master. His sister was his masters
daughter–became enciente by her father & master & was sold to
a sporting man in Tennessee. I know enough of him to make an
Uncle Toms Cabin. Advise him well, & may God prosper him.

Your aff Uncle Erastus

XI

Saving Things — "Heaven but lends,
never gives to Earth"

I AM SLOWLY TRANSCRIBING THE VARIOUS LETTERS I have copied
from the MHS, Historic Northampton and the Duke Archives. I work on an old cherry drop leaf table that we had
in the kitchen of our Kansas City house for the seven years that
Peter worked there. We bought it from an antique dealer soon
after we arrived and it quickly became the seat of all work and
much conversation in our little bungalow. I love the velvety patina
of this table, and all its tiny scars bearing witness to scribblers
before me. It has been carefully restored, probably more than
once, but it has kept its soft buttery character. The dealer who
sold it to us declared that it was made in the eighteenth century
in Ipswich, Massachusetts, a tiny village that keeps threading its
stories back into mine. Two branches of my family began their
American life here. Nettie and Caro went to school there. And for
an added flourish, John Updike wrote many of his novels there,
maybe on one of these drop leaf tables.

Erastus writes to Nettie and Caro in 1863:

> *Here I am at my library table bending nearly double to the task*
> *of writing to you—steel bowed open on my nose—in grey vest*
> *& pants & white shirt sleeves. There is a little gabbler in the*
> *hall just going off with mamama under the trees [a reference*
> *to Sadie, his now three-year-old granddaughter, Swinton's*
> *daughter]. My table is strewed as usual with other folks things*
> *& my room is open to the public. The distant voices of Lizzie &*

Sarah echo from the. . .shades of the building. All else is still, save
the monitory moans of menacing thunder. The sky is overcast
and the waters are gathering to descend upon the thirsty earth.

Where is that library table is now? Burned as kindling? A
worktable in someone's basement? Or carefully polished and
preserved, the treasured centerpiece of someone's contemporary
study? Our relationship to "stuff" changes with each generation.
Maybe sometime in the distant past there was a generation or
a culture that was as hungry for stuff as this one has been, but
it's hard to imagine that coming to pass without the incessant
harping of powerful advertisers who tell us today of our deep
need for more. When my paychecks stop and I start living on my
savings, I look around and notice that I have everything I could
ever need. Just like those Boston ladies who "have their hats," I
have mine. The deep recession that George Bush left us in has
made the most unexpected people come to the same conclusion.
Enough stuff. Let's polish up what we've got and look at it with
new eyes.

In the history museum business "stuff" is the heart and soul
of the institution. When I first entered that profession, I was
overwhelmed with the desire to collect everything I could lay
my hands on because my imagination could invest the smallest
things with huge meaning. When I wanted to honor a board
member, I would wrap up a hundred-year-old dime in a velvet
pouch and present it with a story spun from the characters who
had designed it, forged it, and the hundreds of laboring immigrants, excited children, and high-born ladies who had held it in
their hands for a moment, for whom it might have represented
their food for the day, or a child's future piece of candy. Even the
smallest, simplest object has a story to tell that usually can only
be imagined. A tough teenage boy once held a little piece of
scrimshaw in the attic collection space of my museum and after
sitting with it for fifteen minutes wrote a story of the killing of
the whale to get the ivory, of the boredom that led to the carving,
of the characters carved, black and white, in little oar boats, of

the markets they served and the light they brought through the harvested oil. With a willing imagination, a story of ecology, humanity, economics and art, all in one small piece of ivory.

Peter buys most of his clothes from Charlie Davidson at the Andover Shop in Cambridge (socks always come from J.C. Penney). One day I go with him and Charlie shows me Peter's "book." Every jacket, suit or pair of pants he's bought in thirty years is recorded there, with a swatch of the material and his exact measurements, a tale of good eating. It is a fat book, and Charlie has them for hundreds more people, the luminaries of Cambridge, individually captured in a timeline of their tweeds and expanding waistlines. Oh, how I would like to have Erastus's "book" with a swatch of that velvet collared jacket he wears in his forties and the grey vest and pants of his solitary working days. I want to reach out and touch him.

I have solved the mystery of who sold the William Swinton Bennett Hopkins papers to Duke. I knew that Duke had bought them in 1983 from Seaport Autographs in Mystic, Connecticut. When Googled, Seaport Autographs pops up right at the top of the page. I send along an email inquiry. It doesn't take long for a reply to bounce back into my mailbox from Norman Boas who says, yes, he remembers the letters he sold to Duke very well. They were among a much larger collection of more than five hundred letters he had bought at a local auction, a sack of yellowed, handwritten letters, long unread, auctioned off as a mystery bag. He and his wife, Doris, had spent two years reading and cataloguing them. They were from the estate of William Appleton Aiken and those that were of keen interest to him related to President Franklin Pierce and his wife Jane, whose sister was Aiken's grandmother. But William Appleton Aiken was also Erastus's great grandson, the child of Swinton's second daughter Elizabeth Peck Hopkins. And so the letters that Swinton had saved from his sisters and his parents and friends over the years had made their way into this massive garbage bag of material that

Norman Boas bought on a summer day in 1980. When I look up William Appleton Aiken I find that he was an English Professor at Lehigh University who died quite young. The University of Michigan has his papers. The thing that strikes me is that he was born in Worcester, in March 1907, the same city and the same month as my father. They were second cousins, they both graduated from Yale in 1929, and they surely knew each other.

I can hear a little change in his voice when Norman Boas learns that my interest is Erastus Hopkins.

"I actually have an oil painting of him. I bought it at the same sale, quite damaged, and I've never gotten around to doing anything with it, but it's quite good. If you want it, you can have it for what I paid, $150."

My heart lurches at this speech. Another God-siting, as Gloria White Hammond would say. Boas goes and gets the portrait and describes the damage to me in detail on the phone. "It's signed James Harvey Young on the back," he says.

I know just what this portrait is. In my newspaper research I have found a small article that says that the Connecticut River Railroad had commissioned the portraits of their four presidents in 1866, Erastus included. The artist was James Harvey Young, whose work is in many museums in the country, including eleven paintings in the Peabody Essex Museum in Salem, Young's hometown. My breath is catching in my throat at the thought of restoring Erastus's portrait, repairing the tears and wiping away the soot and grime of a hundred and fifty years. Another part of my brain is thinking of what Peter will say. Portraits are a slightly sore subject in our household, since a six-foot portrait of my great grandfather, Nettie's husband, Benjamin Kendall Emerson, has landed on our living room wall, for lack of another house large enough in the family. Though we both agree that it is a gorgeous portrait, it is so powerful a presence that my husband claims a substantial debt is owed to him to tolerate the housing of an in-law. The picture is of an old man in a dusty blue grey suit with a quarry of pink grey stone behind him. In his right hand he holds a pickaxe; his left hand is held low at a forty five degree angle, as though he's quieting an orchestra of cicadas out in the desert. He has a full white beard and the bright blue eyes of all our family. If you look closely you can see a Phi Beta Kappa key on a gold chain hanging from out of his pocket. My father gave me that beautiful engraved key when I earned a much more modest rendition in college. A friend once looked at the portrait and whispered to me "Ah, there's your rock." B.K. Emerson was the chairman of the Geology Department at Amherst College for nearly half a century.

I drive down to Mystic on a beautiful fall afternoon and find my way into a secluded community in a vast marsh near the Connecticut coast. Norman Boas is a retired medical doctor with a passion for collecting and a special love for President Lincoln. He is the grandson of Franz Boas, the great anthropologist whom I know as the creator of the remarkable museum collection and display on the ground floor of the New York Museum of Natural History. He lives in a recently constructed, very elegant row house in what might be a retirement community. A long road winds through a great flat expanse of golden marsh teeming with wildlife. The marsh comes right up to the deck and large windows make the interior and exterior a seamless domain. Norman has leaned Erastus on a chair in a sun filled alcove. "Are you related to him?" he asks me. "My great-great grandfather," I reply. "What you might call a 'lost relative.' I discovered him through some of his letters that were buried in an archive of the Mass Historical Society and that set me off on a mission to reconstruct his life and understand who he was."

We sit with the October sunlight streaming in over the tea his wife Doris has prepared. We admire Erastus. His portrait leans on a chair between us like a member of the tea party. It has a large, intimidating U shaped tear running on either side of the head and through the beard. It is grimy and dark having probably been in the company of smokers for many years, but it is a very good portrait. Erastus looks out gravely, a much older man than the photograph of him I had found at the MHS, but still handsome, with blue eyes and grey flecking his blond beard and full head of hair. The background suggests a blue and white stripe wallpaper that has been all but obscured by grime but will give interest when the portrait is cleaned.

"I was incredibly lucky to stumble across this amazing bag of letters just down the road at an estate auction," says Norman. "I realized right away that it contained letters from Jane Pierce to her sister and a few from Franklin Pierce. The other manuscripts were secondary to me, but Doris and I spent two years reading all the letters and carefully cataloguing them. They went to a variety of institutions that had appropriate collections. Duke was interested in the Swinton Hopkins letters because of his Southern connections and, of course, they had the funds to buy them." We walk around the house and he shows me some of his own art: a portrait of Lincoln he acquired at the same auction and has had beautifully restored by a man who evaluated Erastus's portrait at the same time and, offered to restore it for three hundred dollars. I am relieved to hear a price for restoration that might be within my means. He also has two stunning bronze busts of his grandfather. "I wrote a biography of my grandfather, " he says, and offers me a copy. We have a common bond in our deep resonance with this kind of personal history, the power of bringing an ancestor into the light of a new generation.

He slides Erastus between two pieces of cardboard he has taped together in advance for protection and hands the two foot square portrait, which had languished in his basement for so long, back into family hands. As I drive back to Boston the ochre light turns into a pink dusk and then darkness. The steady gaze of my fellow passenger behind me is the other beam in the evening. Erastus has my back.

The portrait discovery occurred in the same fall as my first painting class. I have raised two artists (painting and ceramics), am married to one (theater) and have a son-in-law who is a painter in the style of Caravaggio. But I have always been a word person: left-brained. My drawings look much like they did when I was four, though I have moved on in subject matter. Then I only drew one thing: a bed, sideview, with a woman in it—my mother who lay dying in the sunroom of our house for a year when I was five. I drew that picture everywhere, on every book fly leaf and every scrap of paper I could find. I come across these strange little images occasionally when I open my tattered old *Charlotte's Web* or *Stuart Little*. When I finished visually processing my dying mother in her bed, I gave up drawing for the next fifty years.

One day I begin to do exercises to try to see the lines and shadows of what I am trying to draw, rather than the object itself. I painstakingly copy pictures upside down and draw flowers without looking at the paper I am drawing on, using the instructions given in Betty Edwards' *Drawing on the Right Side of the Brain*. And gradually I get a little better. I take a watercolor course. I take my watercolors with me when I travel and start painting in my spare time instead of shopping. One day I am painting the view from a terrace of a hotel and a man who has been watching me for an hour asks if he can buy my painting. I sell him three, which he takes home to Virginia to frame.

In my childhood home I can remember no talk of beauty. My father, a scientist and doctor, saw things from the perspective of their utility. I never heard him comment on anything being beautiful or ugly. He just didn't see that way. And so, as a young person, I didn't either. I know from Erastus's writing that he felt the poetry of the world and I wonder where he had learned to see that way and express himself. He writes to Nettie and Caro at school:

"The sky is overcast & the waters are gathering to descend upon the thirsty earth. The waters above the firmament, & the waters beneath the firmament are about to meet each other, & every watery surface round about is to dance with sweet kisses as it

greets the rain drops from the skies, which a kind Providence distills. These waters from above will flow for awhile on their earthly course, til God's sunbeams gently lift them back to heaven. Heaven but lends, ne'er gives to earth. Some drops of water hang for an hour on the leaves & the grasses, & ne'er touch the grosser earth, and their history here is written in the words "sparkled, were exhaled; & went to heaven." How like the history of Maria, Willie, Lottie & Johnnie! Other drops reach the ground and mingle with its impurities & then have to pass many dark hours & days to be filtered through earth & rocks and yawning caverns—to be broken over stones and waterfalls ere they pass up again to heaven. Such is life prolonged on earth. But the waters are never more beautiful & radiant than when torn & broken into spray they reflect the rainbow hues of the light from above. These represent those heaven born ones whose souls are torn & broken & ground to powder by afflictions, working in them the development of every Christian grace. The flower, when crushed, gives forth its sweetest odor."

The letter calls to mind a renaissance painting, with little winged people floating up to heaven, a radiant dove showing the way. I think of *The Assumption of the Virgin* by Titian, hanging for four hundred years in the Frari Church in Venice. I imagine that when he was on his honeymoon in Rome in 1841 Erastus stood and gazed at a few Titians, Michaelangelos, and Fra Angelicos. They don't call Rome the eternal city for nothing.

XII

Crumbs around a Far Off Table

LINC AND I HAVE NOW EXCHANGED SEVERAL LETTERS. His come about ten days after I mail mine. It's as though we are counting the silent beats in a score of music, taking great care not to come in too soon. Neither of us wants to put too much pressure on this delicate thing we have created. His last letter described a telephone conversation with his parents in which they advised him, and he agreed, that he must keep up with his medication and above all get along and control his aggression. He has now served six years in isolation in Massachusetts, for assaults he has committed while in the prison system. Until these are resolved in the courts of the Commonwealth he will not be moved to North Carolina, the jurisdiction of his original crime. Ultimately he will have to serve a sentence of six years for manslaughter in the south.

He says he is looking forward to getting on with things, to getting to North Carolina into the general prison population. He paints a picture for me of how he will get along with the other prisoners and the guards and control his temper. Of how maybe they will let him work on a farm outside. He will take correspondence courses and complete his college education. Then he imagines he will get out after about six years and maybe sell *The Boston Globe* in supermarkets. He sounds upbeat and hopeful. He implores me to visit him.

For weeks I make half-hearted attempts to find the right contact numbers at the jail. The prospect of upping our relationship from pen pals to face-to-face contact makes me feel like a knot is being pulled tight around my heart. But I am also curious. I have visited the inside of the South Bay Prison in Boston and the Plymouth House of Correction in the past decade, once with an acquaintance who is a guard and once as part of the organization Lead Boston. I have written an article for *The Boston Globe* on prison history in the city and the layers of confusion we have about whether we are punishing or reforming our inmates. Not so long ago I arranged for a photographer to record the last days of the Charles Street Jail for the city's historical society. The photos were horrific. The Jail is spiffed up now as the Liberty Hotel and its bar is called the Clink. The Speaker of the Massachusetts House of Representatives just held a fundraiser there. We do not wish to inhabit a landscape of sorrow, so we just obliterate it.

I send the piece of me that can be clinical out to find the number. The number Linc has given me doesn't penetrate deep enough into the system to get the job done. I leave messages on his parents' machine but they are in Florida. Finally I get an email from his mom with the information and set up a visit through Assistant Superintendent Desiree Lashley to whom I take a great liking. I have to give her my license and social security numbers so she can check me out, and then she calls back to tell me I've been cleared. I think about taking my nine-month-old granddaughter, Margaret, on a Monday when she is in my care. Linc has two nieces who visited him last month who are the same age. The three girls will be a very lively cohort at our shared summer home in Maine for many years to come and I imagine he'd get a kick out of seeing the third member of the triumverate. My secondary motive is to take the pressure off the conversation if it turns out to be awkward. Desiree says, "Fine, bring her, but just be aware you can't take anything else into the room with you—no diapers, bottles, rattles." "Barebottomed?" I ask in my fathomless ignorance. Margaret decides the question by getting a touch of bronchitis on the appointed day. So I go alone.

It's the last day of March, 2009, the morning sun sparkling off the Charles as I drive along Memorial Drive heading toward the Middlesex County jail. My eyes keep tearing up as I'm driving. This takes me by surprise. I have been keeping my emotions very under control up to this point, but suddenly I am flooded with images of Linc as a little boy playing with Hannah. Grinning like a drunken man-in-the-moon as he dumps sand in her bucket. Just your average toddler, but filled with love from every corner of his family. In my mind I hug Eamon and Margaret hard to me to protect them from adulthood.

I get to the jail and realize my next problem will be parking because at this moment I have an injured foot. I have a stress fracture and can't walk very well with my big boot. It's all permit parking but when I come back around the block there's my space, right out front. Two hours for free. I'm thinking like Erastus now: God is with me. I stop for a little prayer to thank him and to ask him to fill me with the Holy Spirit for the next hour.

The security guards at the front door look at me quizzically and tell me that usually visiting hours are only on the weekends. I have an appointment, I tell them, and they pass me through the metal detectors and send me up to the 17th floor control room. Slow elevators. The control room is a dreary bathroom-tiled, big empty space for the visiting public with a wall of lockers. It's echoingly empty. A large guard booth area sits behind bullet-proof glass and a guard looks out at me but keeps on with his business. There is a sign on the window that says "Any removal of undergarments will be grounds for the suspension of visiting privileges." I'm a little slow, but it finally dawns on me what that's all about. The guard slips a green form into a sliding drawer, like a bank teller uses, and I fill it out with all the same information I have provided on the phone. They now have all they need to steal my identity, I think to myself. Assistant Superintendent Desiree

Lashley appears at my elbow. She is a beautiful black woman who exudes an aura of intelligence and assurance, and her presence gives me comfort. She takes on the role of my guide and mentor, helps me with the locker, the metal detector and guides me into the visitor room on the other side of the glass guard booth. I sit down at the middle of three windows and realize that I can hardly see over the window ledge. She laughs, "Oh everyone has that problem— this is how they solve it." And she puts another green plastic chair on top of the first, so that now my feet are swinging like a toddler's, but at least I can see in the window.

I have a strategy for my conversation with Linc which is to listen and keep priming the pump so he will talk. To be a friend and a witness. I am curious right now about Desiree Lashley.

"You must get to know all these guys pretty well," I hazard.

"Oh yes, I know them all right. I've been here for twenty years." She rolls her eyes. "How long since you've seen him?" she asks me.

"Seven years." She makes a little warning gesture with her eyes, as if to say: "You're in for a surprise, get yourself prepared." What she really says is: "Normally visits are about a half hour, but I'll let you have some extra time."

As he will inform me early in our conversation, he's been incarcerated for exactly five years and eleven months, but I hadn't seen him for a while before that. My real relationship with Linc was when he was a child; rebellious teenage boys don't have much interest in aunts. (Though he is my cousin, our relationship is more like an aunt to a nephew and he calls me Aunt Anne.) Linc started acting out in his early teens, in various ways that I was not privy to at the time. His family sent him to the Hyde School, a private school that involves the whole family in a twelve-step program. It was intense and went on for years. Then one day he ran away from the school with a classmate named Jane. Next thing we knew they were married and she was pregnant. I only met Jane once and she seemed to be in a permanent rage at everything and everyone who crossed her path. Now

I understand that this is a manifestation of a manic episode in a bipolar life. Linc's parents were devastated but tried to make the best of the situation. In the end she took up with another man and they got divorced. Noah, their little boy, would come to visit his father and grandparents occasionally, but Jane had him most of the time.

Desiree Lashley leaves me alone to contemplate the room and wait for Linc's delivery. In front of me is a black telephone receiver, with a matching one on the other side of the glass. Each of the three windows is smeared with the ghostly imprint of a palm, people reaching out to touch each other. They are fresh. It must happen with almost every visit. I look away. Within a few minutes I see Linc round the corner with a guard on his elbow. He enters the tiny tiled room on the other side of the glass and the guard leaves us. I am completely startled at how he has aged. His hair has turned quite grey and is very close cropped. His brown eyes are popping wide, intense. He smiles and says "Aunt Anne." I can hear him fairly well through the glass, but he gestures to the phone and we both pick up. I start. "Hi. Did you know I was coming?"

"Well I knew you were coming sometime, but not today exactly. Thank you so much for visiting." He gave me a big smile and his eyes held on to mine like a magnet.

"I'm very pleased to visit you Linc, and I've loved your letters." I ask him about what I was most curious about. "Tell me about your saga through the system. What different places have you been in and what has it been like?" He launches right into his story without missing a beat.

"I've been incarcerated for five years and eleven months. I've been in Bridgewater, Billerica, and here, the Middlesex House of Corrections, twice. It all started from something Jane said on the phone. It made me think that her boyfriend was molesting the kids [Noah, Linc's son, had a half sister and brother]. I just got on a bus in Boston and went all the way to North Carolina. Took a taxi to the house. Philip was alone with the kids and I confronted him. He denied it of course, and we got into a fight."

Linc had been a champion wrestler in high school. "He was a hellava big guy. I got him into a headlock. I just kept squeezing," he said. "I went too far." I had heard all this from his family at the time but hearing it from him brought me tight into that circle of fury and then panic he must have felt. "I didn't want the kids to see, so I hid his body behind the couch." I knew that Noah had seen and I thought we'd better clear this up so I asked him directly.

"Did Noah see you?"

"Well he saw me on top of Philip. Finally I put the body in the attic. But Jane knew something was up the minute she came home and she asked the kids "Did Linc kill Philip?"

"I just wanted to go out and clear my head. I wasn't thinking clearly. I thought we should just go out and get a bite to eat and figure out what to do next. I got in the truck and Jane called the police. So I called the police too. But I should have called the police myself right away." This is a side of Linc I know, the side that says what he thinks you want to hear.

"You weren't in control of yourself. You must have panicked," I offered.

"Yeah...so they took me to the jail and I was there for five months. Then I was flown home because my parents had arranged for me to be evaluated at McLean Hospital." He describes the plane trip and taking some prescription medications that got him so sped up that he didn't sleep for twenty-four hours.

"I should have told my parents that I wasn't in good shape to get evaluated, but I went anyway. They shipped us all over the place at McLean and we were waiting out in a corridor and a janitor came by with a mop and pail and bumped into my mom. I just went ballistic. Got him in a headlock. And I used the N word." He looked down. "I shouldn't have said that."

We talked for over an hour. It turned out that he had been involved in at least two other assault incidents in this jail during a previous stay. One of them happened with a guard who had taken away all his books. When his lawyer came for a visit and his shackles were removed, Linc flew at the guard in a fury and pummeled him. It would turn out that the guard, despite his football player's physique, would get a full disability pension out of this encounter. It would take six years of solitary confinement before all these Massachusetts charges would be settled. Six years before he would go to North Carolina to begin serving the manslaughter charges.

I keep thinking they are going to chase me away, or take Linc, and I don't want the visit to end abruptly. It is clear that Linc didn't want it to end at all. At one moment when the conversation pauses he tells me the detailed plot of the first 122 pages of a Ken Follett novel, hoping to keep my interest. I ask him about his life here. He is in an 8x10 cell with a "canteen." When I read his letters I was picturing the canteen as a place where you went for a snack, kind of like camp. No, it is more like a minibar in a yellow tiled cell, without the alcohol. Peanuts and Fritos and Coke that he can eat when he wants. He is allowed out in the recreation area from 10 to 11 pm, when all the other prisoners are in their cells and he can be alone. All his meals are brought to him in his cell.

"They're not bad," he says when I ask about the meals. "Today I had Italian sausage for lunch."

It's only 11 am. He is on the most secure floor, in "segregation," where they monitor the most dangerous prisoners, or those most in danger of being severely molested by other prisoners, like child rapists. I think, from a newspaper account that I have read, that one of his assault charges is against one of these child rapists. He tells me all this and says that he says hi to the others as he walks by their cells, but he doesn't know them. We talk about his meds and his "treatment." He's on Resperdal, an anti-psychotic medication, and he tells me that he knows he must stick with it, that he has to conquer his aggression. He gets no regular psychiatric visits. I can see from his eyes that he's full of anxiety. In this month's *New Yorker* magazine there's an article on the brain destruction caused by isolation in torture camps and prison. Keeping anyone in isolation is cruel and unusual punishment, against the eighth amendment. Keeping a schizophrenic there is a guarantee that he will get worse.

We talk about his cousins and what they are doing. Of our shared family place in Maine and how complicated it has become to deal with our ever increasing numbers. Of his childhood interest in painting. Of his poetry. Of his son, who has every promise of being a happy person and a good musician. Linc is a good conversationalist, knows how to keep my attention. I am actually enjoying myself.

He talks most of all about getting on with the serving of the sentence. He says that Jane sent him a picture of her new baby and she will visit him when he gets to North Carolina. She's three hours away and that counts as far and qualifies for a full day visit. I cringe a little at thinking he is still involved with this woman. His parents now have full custody of Noah and are raising him. "How many kids does Jane have?" I ask.

"Six, counting the new baby."

"And how many are in her custody?"

"Oh, just the new one. All the rest are either in the custody of grandparents or their fathers." I think there are four fathers, but I don't ask.

Linc recites to me all the reasons he has to be grateful and optimistic. I ask him if it would be alright for me to say a prayer for him, out loud. I tell him that I've been going to a church where I've learned to do this, though I'm still a beginner. I assure him that it won't mean the end of our visit, but that I'd like to do it before they make me leave. So I begin "Heavenly Father, we are in awe of your power and presence in our lives. We praise you. I ask you to lift up my cousin Linc, Lord, to surround him with your presence and the Holy Spirit." At the end I tell Linc about Adoration, Contrition, Thanksgiving and Supplication, the ACTS acronym, that I had learned as the framework for prayer. His eyes bore into me and he said, "Say that again, I want to remember it." Then he repeats it back to me four or five times. A man hungry for any tools of survival.

A guard eventually puts his head in and says it is time to end the visit. We pantomime a hug through the glass as I get ready to leave, and Linc blows me a kiss. I assure him I will return. On my way out I look down at the cast on my broken foot and realize I haven't thought about it for more than an hour.

★ ★ ★

I wish Erastus was still around, still writing. I am searching his letters for one that might bring Linc some cheer. They are so full of domestic comfort, the very thing he is most lacking. And admonitions to do right, something he has lost his main opportunity to do. Still, he reports to me that he is very focused on the idea of doing right—and keeping control. So maybe I'll send him this one:

Northampton February 9, 1862 Sabbath PM

My Dear Little Chicks,

I think the eyes and mouths of stranger beholders would open wide if they beheld the portly damsels whom I call "chicks." But then you are so. You are the only ones I have though you do pick up crumbs around a far off table. Yes you are dear and precious to me; and when you grow into womanhood- so rapidly approaching- I shall feel my work on earth accomplished- that I have no other chicks to live for, and am ready to depart to another world.

But I am anxious you shall grow up right, and the first requisite of this is that you bow yourselves, your will, your very thought to the will & wish of God. If you wish to be happy, do just right; & if you wish to do just right all the time & in everything—go to God every day—as you would go to Mama in the next room—and assured of his veritable presence and hearing, ask him with all sincereity & solemnity to show you what is right & then do it, at whatever sacrifice. Now please, will you my darlings, comply with this request.

Nettie, you are the youngest, and if I did not know that Caro was kind and gentle, I would not say you ought to regard her wishes greatly in larger and in lesser things. Now just turn your eyes and see that coat thrown on the bed—those shoes sprawling round—that book left in the chair etc and put them all up. This is right, and to be good and happy you must do right.

And so you, Caro, be kind and gentle, as I know your heart will tell you, to your younger sister. Learn to subject your wish and will to your superiors, and as you have no mama, or elder sister to claim precedence over you, practice on Uncle Charles to be deferential, yielding and compliant with his views and wishes, if it does not cost a sacrifice. I trust you do not need this admonition, and I do not believe you do, but then I want to give you some good advice, and I know of none better.

How time flies! You will soon be here. Make haste then with your studies and have some advance in knowledge to show for all the privileges you have enjoyed and all the sacrifices we accept on your accounting... And now, my darlings, reluctantly and with a yearning for some undiscovered way to express to you my tender affection, I am your fond

Father

It is hard to know how this letter might make Linc feel. Maybe he is just humoring me in saying he really likes reading them. They make my letters longer and fatter and that's a good thing I think. So I will continue, and I will ask him what he thinks about when he reads them. I talked to his oldest sister after my visit and she expressed great relief that he's now on his medications and in a state to be visited. He was quite frightening to her a year ago.

★ ★ ★

I have been sharing my writing output with six relative strangers every two weeks since September. In earlier times of my life I have been in writing groups, but this one is different: an inspired and professional leader, and a very unusual group of writers. Two of my fellow writers are way ahead of me in their spiritual education, having been raised as Catholics. Catholics, I discover, have deep wells of writing material, on both sides of the spiritual divide.

Patti, who writes stunning meditations on swimming in cyberspace and at night in the Ipswich River, suggests I read a particular work of Thomas Merton. At home I look in my bookshelf and find Merton's *No Man is an Island*, another work of his, and open it at random.

> "God's will is a profound and holy mystery, and the fact that we live our everyday lives engulfed in this mystery shouldn't lead us to under estimate its holiness. We dwell in the will of God as in a sanctuary....God's will is more than a concept. It is a terrible and transcendent reality, a secret power which is given to us, from moment to moment, to be the life of our life and the soul of our soul's life...it is a creative power, working everywhere, giving life and being and direction to all things and above all forming and creating, in the midst of an old creation, a whole new world which is called the Kingdom of God."

It is Easter week. My favorite holiday of the year. We have six childen under six and seven more children under fifty coming to hunt for eggs in the yard and eat barbecued leg of lamb. I love this combination of pagan festival of fertility mingled with the resurrection. Something for everyone—so cleverly parallel in meaning.

XIII

No hand but my own

DRY BONES KEEP SHOWING UP IN MY LIFE. My first encounters were in the plays of August Wilson: Harold Loomis's vision in Joe Turner's *Come and Gone*, and Citizen's spiritual journey to the City of Bones in *Gem of the Ocean*. The reference is from *Ezekiel* 37 where the Lord leads Ezekiel to a valley full of dry bones, after Israel is taken by the Babylonians. He commands him to prophesy and to bring the bones to life, which Ezekiel obediently does. It is one of the most stunning images of the Bible, the vast rattling of thousands of bones as they rise and come together and are given flesh. To some African Americans these are the bones of their ancestors, and as they collectively inch their way to justice in our society they hear them rattling.

I feel a little like Ezekiel who, when asked by the Lord if he thought the bones could come to life, answered, "If you would have it so." Erastus's dry bones seem to have been given new life in me, and given me new life, so where do I go from here? Thomas Merton minces no words about God's will. A terrible and transcendent reality and a secret power given to us. To use. I am meditating on this as I prepare Easter dinner for thirteen beloved children and grandchildren. It is spring at last. Winters get longer and longer as I get older and my longing for the light and color of spring grows more intense each year, like the longing for a beloved person. It is almost as though I am becoming spring, folded into nature, a kind of personal resurrection. And at the same time comes a feeling that I am preparing to be folded back into creation. This feeling is nothing new, but the intensity of it is.

On Easter Eve I write a letter to a dying college friend who has bravely endured a kidney transplant only to get pancreatic cancer. The transplant failed and she has made the choice to go off dialysis, which means she will not be with us when I get back from my trip to Italy in three weeks. This is the first of my friends to go and I know we are entering a new season. I write to her and include some words of comfort drawn from those imparted by Erastus to his children.

When I return from Rome she has gone.

I have been reading Erastus's "late" letters. I find it painful to know that I will come to the end of his correspondence. He is so alive to me. I dread his dying, the silencing of his voice. These boxes of letters without him will be cavernously dull. I know the fact: he will die of "paralysis" in January, 1872, apparently from a series of strokes at the end of his life. There is no treatment for heart disease in this era. But surely he will face his own death with a calm assurance, the angelic faith of his dear Caro. This is the faith that he had instilled in her and whose truth she made visible to him in her last moments. He knows he will be with her, and all the others who have gone before him.

In 1869 and 70 the family goes with him to Heidelberg and Dresden, on a trip apparently taken because of his failing health. His handwriting is tiny and trembling.

October 5, 1869, Heidelberg

My Dear Sadie,

I do not like to write to any of my dear friends with any other hand than my own, for it seems as if they would love to read it better in my own writing & with their own eyes. But I will try Mamama's hand. It is just as dear a hand as anybody's—and

oh how many kind things it has done for you and for your papa
when he was a very little boy; it is the dear hand which I once
thought, & now think so lovely. But I will tell it what to say.

He describes their trip down the Rhine. His love itself seems
to grow through its tender expression in his letters, like the exercise of a muscle. As Peter and I get on a plane to go to Rome
the woman behind me calls her children on the phone and reads
them two chapters of an adventure story before we take off. I
listen raptly, as if I were curled up in my pajamas beside her. This
is the modern way to touch far off children: she wants to stay
connected, to touch down in their world before bedtime. Connection is the conundrum of the modern age. Solitude is a siren
pleasure in my life and I find it takes enormous effort to keep connected in the world. I sometimes feel like a helium balloon and I
hope some hand will hang on to my string. Could it be that this
is a dysfunction of the amygdala, that place in the brain for the
processing and memory of emotional reactions? Or that a piece
of me wandered off when my mother died, searching for her?
Travelling legitimizes this disconnecting. For a time we can shelve
our own identity, and float entirely in the present moment.

We touch down in Rome on a beaming April afternoon at 2
p.m. My body clock has lurched forward six hours and I am suddenly awake. We collect our luggage and seek out the train to the
city. All the automatic ticket dispensers at the airport train station
are standing there with their guts removed and the line to buy a
ticket is deep and wide, Italian style. The train company has "out-
sourced" their ticket selling operation and the simple machines
that worked so well are now part of the archeological landscape.
I call Paolo DiMedici, our apartment agent, while Peter queues.
We climb on the train with our suitcases, my fat backpack, his
Colombian leather bag and my French easel, in its red carrying
case with the backpack straps I have stripped off a thrift store
backpack and attached with many crisscrossing lines of thread,
hoping they will hold. We travel light, but with books and computers and painting supplies, it's still a heavy load.

Since February I have been painting almost every day, sometimes for eight hours at a stretch. I have such a pressing need to paint, that I will paint almost anything: moldy fruit, old photographs that I've taken years ago, one of the two of us eating in a restaurant in Siena. I take one adult education course which gives me the basic idea that you need certain colors, that there are complementary colors and that you mix them in certain ways, that you use "medium" which seems to be any of a variety of substances that you mix with paint to make it workable on a canvas, that you need to clean your brushes properly. Our teacher is younger than my children and still in school herself. She has us paint from pictures in a magazine that she brings in. The woman next to me spends the first three classes copying in pencil a photograph of a man crossing a doorway in a Tunisian souk, in preparation for her painting. By the time she is ready to paint I have finished three very bad paintings.

Then I go spend a day with my son-in-law Sean, who paints everyday, all day, and is a brilliant craftsman and a very successful artist. He has very generously allowed me to come paint beside him and has set up a simple still life in his beautiful studio in Woodstock, Connecticut. Three peaches, some grapes, a fat jug and a blackberry. His fruit is a little moldy too, but it doesn't matter. Seven hours later, no lunch or bathroom break, I have created my first real painting. I have learned an incredible amount. About shadow and color and brush strokes and composition. But I know that I should not impose on Sean too often. I go home and do six more paintings, none of which are quite finished. I will finish them when I learn more.

I go one day to see my friend George Nick, a painter whose work I love, who specializes in painting outdoors in winter light from his red truck, in which he has cut a window so he can paint in comfort. He looks at my work and sees where there is energy and composition. He talks to me about the process of painting. I am beginning to understand that there are as many ways to paint as there are painters in the world. A very liberating idea. Just paint. Find out what the paint will do. George may work on a painting for four months, but he works on several at a time in natural light for a relatively brief time each day. Sean works in a studio set up for a constant light and works on a single painting for three or four days.

So many of my images of Italy are from paintings. When I imagine Erastus and Charlotte in Rome, I see them wandering through a dusty Forum with a few sheep munching on the occasional blade of grass. Right out of a Hubert Robert painting. As I arrive in Rome I am also imagining their entry into the city, after weeks at sea, mightily relieved to get off the boat, swaying slightly for days. But no jet lag. Like us they must have discovered that some things work brilliantly in Italy and others are strangely, permanently broken, like our gutted ticket machine that whispers the news of another private deal. Romans have been learning crafty ways with foreigners for many centuries. Erastus probably made this discovery with his first transaction, getting his steamer trunk onto a carriage bound for the city.

We travel forty minutes on the train to Trastevere station, a route that suggests not an ancient city as much as a modern global wasteland, smeared with the same kind of spray painted graffiti that screams at you in New York, walls of crushed automobiles dividing the landscape. Giant apartments buildings house the regular workers of Rome, who have given over their city to throngs of tourists. In the 1840s it would have been dirty and poor, a Papal State. No frivolity, a place alive with Catholic spirit and the ancient Roman empire. Erastus's interest in the archeology must have outweighed any anti-Catholic sentiments he had, sentiments that were prevalent in Massachusetts at the time. We arrive at Trastevere and load our luggage into a taxi to go to our apartment near the Campo di Fiori. The Campo is closing up its open air market for the day; Giordano Bruno, burned here for heresy in 1600, stands somberly in bronze looking down on a box of rotten eggplant in a small sea of scattered pea pods as we make our way through.

Paolo, the house agent, is waiting for us at 122 Via Monserrato which auspiciously turns out to be next to our favorite Roman fish restaurant, Pier Luigi. I have picked this apartment on the internet because it has an elevator and a small terrace and the price and location are right. But you never know what little ticks any particular place will have, so I am relieved to find it full of light, with a simple modern kitchen, and a bed that will foster togetherness. We say goodbye to Paolo and take a nap.

Peter, recovering from a bad cold, takes a much longer nap than I. I let him sleep and take a walk around the neighborhood. We have a small supermarket around the corner where I buy coffee and cheese and salami. I am looking for a place to paint, which requires something I can compose into an interesting painting and someplace to sit while I paint it. Preferably not in the midst of a throng of people since I am still at a stage that would be dubbed "primitivo" in Italian. Nevertheless, I am determined to improve. I have discovered in painting something that calms me and absorbs me for hours.

In front of the supermarket is a bench looking out on a strange square. There is a news kiosk (very paintable), and a wonderful array of colorful buildings. It is the intersection of five streets so the buildings are going off in every direction. The ground slopes in that curious Roman way that suggests they just slathered over something when they built this little corner. What is beneath us to create this strange mound? I later read that this Square of Montello was some kind of demolition dump during the war, described in the guidebook as "curiously desolate." I have imagined my painting: in my mind I am like Raoul Dufy, creating a collection of buildings with their own lively personalities and angles, quite independent of the rules of perspective. I sit on the bench and begin to sketch on my canvas board. Before long it begins to rain, a rain that will be with us for the next fourteen days. So I go inside to begin my painting, periodically coming out into the wet to reexamine the scene. My bench is now almost always occupied by North African men; I think there is a shelter in the neighborhood. On the last morning I can paint, the sun shines for an hour and I rush out to see how the scene has changed. My little square has been transformed into the Dufy painting I had imagined, with light bouncing off the windows and shutters and hiding under the eaves of these cheerful, shabby buildings.

In the next two weeks I will do two more paintings, in Ostuni and Venice. I am humbled in this process, these are very complex subjects to paint and the light has not behaved. In Venice I paint outside the door of our little apartment, trying to capture the canal and the three church domes in the distance, with crowds of schoolchildren peering over my shoulder and shouting the encouraging *"bella, bella, senora."* This is comfortably humbling, one of the pleasures of getting older. The ego has become a sleepy old bear, ready for hibernation, and if I can offer an entertainment for the children and the tourists, that is its own pleasure.

From Rome we take an early morning fast train to the Province of Puglia in the boot of Italy. I stop at the newsstand in the station and buy some postcards and stamps. One for Linc and one for Eamon. It takes me a few days of contemplation before I write to Linc. What must it feel like to get a postcard from so far away, to receive this tangible token of the liberty of other people when you are in solitary confinement without windows or sunlight. I dwell on the rain and the food. For Eamon, the voice of Erastus pours right through my pen as though I were writing to little Sadie.

My twenty-five-year-old Michelin *Green Guide* to Italy doesn't even mention Puglia's existence, but we have been thinking about this trip for a long time. I have picked an in-town villa on the edge of the central park of little Ostuni, which will be our hub for day trips to places like Lecce and Matera. I found it on the internet and have had a charming email conversation with its owner, Gianfranco, for several weeks about practical details and sights to see. Sadly, he will not be one of them as he works in Milan. The train flies through the gray green countryside punctuated by sudden bright yellow fields of rape, the rain streaking across the windows in diagonal streams. We climb down in Ostuni where a young couple have come to fetch us at the station. The town is like a white wedding cake decorated with wisteria on the hill above us, a startling sight. This part of Italy was a Greek outpost for centuries and much that we will see in the next few days will have that whitewashed simple flavor of Greece. Our villa is the elegant old family home of the Auristicci family. It has been divided into three apartments and this one, with an enormous second floor garden, would appear to have been the main living quarters. The entrance on the ground floor feels like the foyer of a French chateau, complete with ceiling cherubs and a giant old clawfooted bathtub (disconnected) in the stairwell. We wish we had friends or family along to share all this with, but we settle into a rhythm together, travelling the countryside, cooking Branzino in a frying pan, playing scrabble, reading in long stretches undisturbed by the chatter of duty.

One day we go to the pretty town of Locorotondo and find ourselves the only diners in one of the village restaurants. The owner, who is also the cook and waiter, insists that we start with the antipasti and starts bringing out plate after plate of eggplant delicacies, artichokes and red peppers, steaming sausages, stuffed mushrooms and zucchinis. Twelve dishes in all. We have this experience several times in Puglia and conclude that perhaps people simply start restaurants out of their village homes in the hopes of snaring an occasional customer. We are early for the tourist season but it is hard to imagine this restaurant doing a booming business even in the peak of summer. But the food is fresh and delicious.

Another day we go to Martina Franca, another hill town with an historic center. As we wander around the rain begins coming down in great sheets and fills the narrow sloping streets with a four inch river gushing downhill. "Streets full of water, please advise," I yell at Peter over the din, a tribute to Robert Benchley's memorable joke telegram about Venice.

But Matera is the high point for me because of Carlo Levi's book, *Christ Stopped at Eboli*. I read it years ago but it seared my mind with its images of poverty. He describes "…that land without comfort or solace, where the peasant lives out his motionless civilization on barren ground in remote poverty, and in the presence of death. 'We're not Christians,' they say. 'Christ stopped short of here, at Eboli.' *Christian* in their way of speaking means *human being*,…and is the expression of a hopeless feeling of inferiority." Levi was banished to Matera Province as a political prisoner in 1935. The town is a startling apparition as we approach. Steeply dug into two hillsides it is a warren of caves with structures built at all kinds of odd angles on top of each other, the roofs of some serving as pathways to others.

The caves of this town are considered to be among the oldest continuously inhabited shelters in Europe, occupied for as long as 9000 years. In *Christ Stopped at Eboli* Levi's sister describes Matera. "As I went by I could see into the caves, whose only light came in though the front doors. Some of them had no entrance but a trap door and a ladder. In these dark holes with walls cut out of the earth I saw a few pieces of miserable furniture, beds, and some ragged clothes hanging up to dry. On the floor lay dogs, sheep, goats, and pigs. Most families have just one cave to live in and there they sleep all together; men, women, children and animals. This is how twenty thousand people live… I felt, under the blinding sun as if I were in a city stricken by the plague." Malaria, trachoma and black fever were constant plagues. Levi's book became the conscience of the Italian nation, and in 1955 the government resettled the entire population in new housing at the top of the hill, but gradually people have crept back and many of the house caves are again inhabited. Now the cave district is eerily gentrified, with a few posh looking hotels created out of a warren of caves.

I return to Boston alone after almost three weeks; Peter is going on to Germany and Austria to festivals of music and dance. He was a professional newspaper critic of both at different times in his life and has a passion and knowledge far beyond mine. Part of me wants to go on with him because I can see and hear so much more in his company. But the other part needs to go home to my garden at this most spectacular moment of the spring. The morning after my late night arrival I come down the stairs and through the French doors see the hundreds of tulips that Eamon and I planted last fall, voluptuous little balls of carmine red on their straight green stems, as if they were strutting dowagers showing off their fancy hats. The crabapple tree above them is an open umbrella of fluffy pink blooms. This is my symphony.

XIV

Love is the Soil from which Anxiety Grows

I HAVE HAD TWO LETTERS FROM LINC since I sent him my paltry postcard from Italy. He has been awaiting his day in court; he is hoping to finish with the assault charges that have accumulated against him in his passage through the prison system in Massachusetts. He has explained each of these episodes to me in some detail. He remembers quite clearly the strange way his mind was working in the moment. But his explanation feels a little coached and walks a wobbly tightrope of contrition and self defense. One time, he tells me, he head butted a guard who was passing because he saw the opportunity to do so and he thought that it was a kind of game: if you got an opportunity, you were supposed to use it. "How stupid of me," he says now.

I decide to visit him again rather than write. After my first visit I wanted to go the next week again, but I stopped myself. I know in the long run I can't sustain that timing and it's not fair to raise his expectations. I call Desiree Lashley and ask if I can come that afternoon. She says she'll have to check on whether there are lawyers coming; she will call me back. She leaves me a message later in the morning: "No lawyers, come on down."

My trip across the river to Cambridge is quite unemotional this time. I find a parking place and walk through the shady courtyard in front of the old brick Bullfinch courthouse. The afternoon is hot for May and has that soft summer sleepiness that makes the humming of bees seem like an overheard conversation. I look up at the twenty-story modern courthouse and prison looming above this tranquil spot and wonder if Linc can see sunlight from his cell. I will ask him.

This time I know the drill. I go through the metal detector and the guard tells me that I will be escorted up to the seventeenth floor. Three guards by the elevator are in a conversation about electronic banking. They would never trust the internet. They get into the elevator with me, without breaking their circle of conversation or making eye contact with me. They are escorting me but also ignoring me. One of them steps out and opens the locked door to the visitor's waiting room on the seventeenth floor. I enter and stand patiently at the control booth waiting for the guard to come over. There's a whiteboard up on the wall that says there are 421 prisoners here today and breaks them down by floor. It lists much smaller numbers for Plymouth, Bridgewater and Billerica which puzzles me. Maybe these are the transfers into Cambridge that are about to happen. There is a video security screen with six views of various parts of the prison, all quiet. A computer screen on the guard's desk has Linc's picture on it, and various fields fill in with information I cannot read. He's a handsome guy, looks like Sean Penn. But here he is prisoner number 4552781, Cambridge postal box 97. This place, with its own eerie, disconnected culture, is his life. Just the elevator ride and my long wait here to be acknowledged gives me a sense of the power dynamics at play with these guards.

I put my pocketbook in the locker, take the metal hairclip out of my hair and put it on the counter with my watch. I go through the metal detector and then come back through to collect my things and go back to sit on the two plastic chairs. I wait for Linc. He comes in to the little room on the other side of the glass looking a little like a skittish deer. He's sleepy, I can see. He is in handcuffs and leg chains. He sits down and holds eye contact with me, smiling, while the guard removes them. Released, he comes over and greets me with a touch of surprise, but also with pleasure. He says he thought I might be his lawyer. I can imagine that he might be a little disappointed. A lawyer can make things happen, bring news one might want to hear.

We talk through the telephones and I can see that he's watching everything that's happening behind me. I finally realize that he's trying to catch the eye of the pretty female guard who's in the control booth. I turn around to look at her. "She's the guard that brings the mail every afternoon," he tells me. And he waves at her with a big smile. He's hungry for her, I can feel his energy right through the glass. For a brief moment I feel intensely uncomfortable in this force field of longing.

"Do they read your mail?" I ask him.

"They open it to make sure there's nothing unusual in it, but I don't think they read it. I loved your postcard from Rome by the way. That fountain is incredible." I am imagining the guards reading my letters and Erastus's aloud in some lounge they sit around in. Linc must be a curious kind of inmate to them— or maybe he's just a number. I wonder if they are scared of him, if he has a reputation for being dangerous.

In his last letter he described playing basketball late at night. I ask him whether he plays with guards or other inmates.

"Most of the guards will play with me, there are a couple who just watch me shoot, but it's really fun when they play. I almost always win, even though I've got handcuffs on. I've kind of learned a special underhand shot." My jaw drops and I mouth "amazing" through the glass.

"Do you talk to any of the other prisoners?" I ask.

"Yeah, I've got a good friend now, Charlie. He's in here because he tricked his business partner and did him out of a lot of money. Charlie's job is to deliver soup to the other guys at night in the cells. He brings me the hot water and dried soup and bowls and I make the soup in my cell and he delivers it to all the guys in the corridor. It's kind of fun."

I find the image of this soup kitchen behind bars kind of endearing and I feel a little sense of relief that Linc has some kind of older, white collar crime friend in here.

On this visit he's quite different than when I saw him a month ago. Jittery, rubbing his neck a lot.

"You seem anxious today," I say.

"Yeah, this medication makes my neck get all tense, and then I can't breathe right. Last night I ran in place for a long time in my cell, trying to work this tension out of my system. I'm anxious all the time. I hate this medication, but I'm under a Roger's order. Do you know what that is? It means if I don't take the medication, they'll strap me down and inject me. I hate that. But my goal is to not take this medication. If I start hearing voices or feeling funny, then I'll take it."

"Maybe they could give you something for the anxiety." I suggest. We talk more about whether he could get to see a doctor. I'm getting a little over my head here, but I can see he needs more help than he's getting. It alarms me to know that he's just waiting to stop taking his medication.

"I'd love to have Hannah come visit me," he says. I know that he's very eager to see this youngest daughter of mine who was his childhood playmate. And that she's very uncomfortable at the thought.

"I think she's working up to it, but she's not quite ready yet. She's dealing with a lot in her own life right now. But I bet she'll be along one of these days." I say evenly. We talk about his son who is being raised by his parents. He is very proud of him and rightly so. He is a handsome teenager and talented musician. I have never seen them together, and I wonder what Noah feels about his father.

I ask him whether he can see sunlight in his cell.

"There's a window on the other side of the corridor from my cell, so I can see it," he says.

A shaft of light conveying all his seasons. A yellow rose glow for summer, a blue grey for winter. Our lives have seasons. In my thirties I was a single mother of two daughters, discovering responsibilities I had not been raised to face. This season in Linc's life should be his summertime, the time that you put in motion the things that will determine how the rest of your life will play out. Work, play, marriage, children. He seems to me a boy in a man's body, innocent of the terrible realities that are still to come. All those longings that will never find fulfillment.

"I have been reading Matthew," he says.

Back at home I begin to think of my next letter to him. He has asked me to send him more of Erastus's letters and I look back to see which I have already sent and which might find some new resonance with him. I pick another of the "school" letters.

Northampton Dec 15 1861

My Dear Children,

You have suffered, I fear, from a dearth of letters, & now you are to have an avalanche of them. I hope that the wolf homesickness has not laid his lacerating fangs upon my dear babes in the wood. I am grieved to hear of the melancholy fate of your poor cousin Lewis—that he had no sooner got fairly away from the sight & scent of his fond nursing mother, & the shade of the first night had hardly gathered around him than the glaring eyes of the fierce demon stared upon him from the midst of the darkness, & the talons of that foe of little children who have first left their mamas were planted in his vitals. Poor Lewis! I hope his sufferings are now ended. I shall always tenderly remember him as the good boy who used to bring the newspapers & ask so affectionately for Nettie and his other cousins.

The news from you has been very gratifying for notwithstanding all the fun you make about the surroundings in the school, it is evident you have got into a real good place where you will have little occasion to think of anything else but that proficiency which you ought to be making. You are in good spirits and have good pluck; & that is half the battle. ...You are very dear to me. When you were little children I had nothing to

do but to enjoy you & to love you, & it was sweet-sweet indeed;
but now that you are getting older, I begin to feel <u>anxious</u> about
you. Love is the soil out of which anxiety grows. Now if a plant
is too rank it exhausts the soil. So when children behave badly, or
even negligently, the anxiety grows apace & tends to exhaust the
love. I have no fear that you will behave badly; but I do fear that
you may be negligent of your opportunities & thus increase my
anxiety & despondency. Please, do not. Let those words clothed
in the silvery tones of a father's love, float ever in your ears &
hear me say, whenever you are tempted to turn aside from the
path of earnest & persistent effort, please, please do not. I shall
not be disappointed or troubled if you are not the best scholars in
school, or if you do not learn as rapidly as some others, but I shall
be sad indeed if you are not just as good & proficient in study
& all things as you can be. That is all. No one can do more than
that, & the one that comes nearest doing the best she can is the
one that deserves the praise & honors of all-the highest rewards.

Your dear Papa.

I know that Linc writes all the time to his son Noah and I am curious to know whether some Erastus-like voice will begin to creep into his letters. Linc has told me that he worries for Noah, that he might be falling into the same distracted wayward activities in school that he was into at the same age.

The day after my visit to Linc, Peter and I fly to California to attend the wedding of his nephew. We have planned a trip that will start in LA and end in San Francisco, visiting with friends along the way, with the wedding midway up the coast, in Cambria. The nephew is marrying the granddaughter of the composer, Arnold Schoenberg, and we are looking forward to meeting their clan. Arriving mid afternoon at the inn, the day before the event, we plunge right into socializing. I am soon exhausted by the chatter of this exceptionally bright group. Peter's siblings are a complicated lot, with halfs and steps and one "real" sister. His sister-in-law has read the recent Atlantic Monthly article on the longitudinal study of the Harvard class of 1941 that points out that a major predictor of lifelong happiness and success is the depth of relationship one has with one's siblings. There is an air of lament that they see so little of each other and that their time to remedy this is getting short. I like each of these people individually but I always get them in a group. At weddings and funerals and holidays: the wasp nests of our lives. I vow to seek them out alone, and to do the same with my own siblings.

In San Francisco we stay with my old friend Julie and her husband David. Julie and I were colleagues thirty-six years ago, had our children at the same time and have stayed in touch sporadically ever since. We have a deep affinity that survives long periods of silence. I look into her strong lined face, framed by long snow white hair and see that we have grown old, a surprising revelation that happens to me like ocean waves, in dashes and retreats. We have both stopped working for pay and are stunned at our happiness, our sense of completion as grandparents and women who deferred many domestic pleasures.

We also share a love of hunting for unacknowledged treasure in thrift shops, auctions and dumpsters. Her house is the quintessence of beautiful taste, with unique and meaningful objects acquired for next to nothing in a lifetime's search. On my last visit she had shown me an old cardboard suitcase, beige with subtle stripes and leather bracing in the corners. "I was in the Salvation Army thrift shop," she said. 'I just felt this beckoning to me. I walked around looking at other things but finally I was compelled to go over and look inside." She opened the suitcase in front of me. It was lined in a satiny beige fabric, with elastic pockets, just like one I had inherited from my mother. "Look in the back pocket," she said. I pulled on the elastic and reached in. A small piece of paper, not much bigger than a calling card, had been left behind by the owner. It was a 1942 order to report to a train station in San Francisco for transfer to an internment camp. It was written in English and Japanese characters. The name of a Japanese family was filled in by hand in ink. The hair stood up on my neck as I looked at it. I had a total body sensation as if my blood was lurching into reverse.

On this visit I read her a couple of letters from Erastus and Julie brings out a small green leather reticule which folds open to reveal a swatch of lace embroidery and a paper pattern. Needles and thimble tucked neatly in the band. Inside is a small piece of paper on which is written in penciled hand: "This was the embroidery reticule of Harriet Rose Chandler who carried it to dancing school on the day she died. She was born in 1847 and was ten years old when she was taken ill. Her sister remembers her well, though she was only five. She was stricken at dancing school with a terrible pain in her bowel and died that day. The doctor later said he thought it was appendicitis." Julie had bought this in an auction lot in Lyme, Connecticut years ago. We looked together at this touching, unusual object and felt the presence of Flora Lincoln, who had written the note, and of little Harriet. We searched for her on ancestry.com and found her. Her father, George, was the head of the State Lunatic Asylum in Worcester, Massachusetts and she lived with her mother, Josephine, and sixty-three inmates, matrons and doctors. Her little sister was not yet born in the 1850 census but every inmate was listed by name and age and profession, if they had one. Like every census record it was full of hidden stories and sadness, softly intimated by this small green sewing box.

I had forgotten that Julie is an outspoken atheist. In our twenties, when we had worked together, I was oblivious to religion. Now I hear Erastus's voice in my ear and I chuckle as Julie expresses her dismay at the powerful hold of religion on all aspects of the renaissance world. We are walking through the Italian painting galleries of the Legion of Honor Museum. I am not inclined to argue though I do point out that it was a brutish and short life at the time, and comfort of any sort must have been welcome. Yesterday Barack Obama spoke in Cairo. "Among some

Muslims there is a disturbing tendency to measure one's own faith by the rejection of someone else's faith...freedom of religion is central to the ability of peoples to live together." I love this president's willingness to say what needs to be said. Julie seems to be doing quite fine without faith. But Linc is another matter. Comfort is needed.

XV

The shortest, sweetest letter ever written

FOR A DECADE I WORKED IN A BUILDING AT HARVARD, once a Sheraton hotel managed by a lanky, shy man named George Scialabba. Quiet and attractive, he sat behind a high desk in the lobby and kept an eye on things in this warren of international research centers. He was usually reading, with an ear cocked for unusual activity. Real bombs had been thrown at some of these researchers in the sixties and now in the nineties we were alert again. He directed visitors to seminar rooms and offices in the upper reaches of the building. We all vaguely knew that he wrote, but we weren't sure what he wrote. We only knew that whatever it was, it had never crossed our paths. So when I turned on my computer the other day and saw a headline on my Arts and Letters Daily homepage that had his name in bold type, I opened the article with great curiosity. It was a review of his book, *What Are Intellectuals Good For?* Ten years after I stopped working with him, I finally got a formal introduction to George.

A reviewer praises him above all because he is not a narrow academic or a gadfly journalist, but a remarkable polymath ranging across disciplines, an obsessive amateur with the time, intelligence, and writing skill to take us touring in the American intellectual landscape. I immediately order his book; it appears that no one has it in stock, but Amazon promises to go search. The review has further revealed to me that in the time I knew this man he was suffering mightily from depression, terrible clinical depression darkened by financial woe.

There is something embarrassing in discovering on the internet, in his own brilliant words, the inner secrets of someone you greeted daily for a decade. In this case it is a dual secret: that George is a brilliant and unique critic whom we all perceived as a clerical worker, and that he was silently suffering in those years, at least some of the time, from depression.

Depression, "the lacerating fang of the wolf," as Erastus would have put it, has sunk its teeth deep into me a couple of times and always taken at least a little bite in August, the month of my mother's death. I am moved when I encounter others who have been through this hell that has shadowed our family. My grandmother was hospitalized with depression several times. My first husband, the father of my children, was chronically depressed and we took turns in our ten-year marriage being immobilized on the couch, staring out the window. When I had my last turn I declared "never again" and I raised my daughters on constant strategic alert for early signs of the impending blues.

Now Hannah has come to live at home with us for a time. This child of mine, such a sturdy funny babe she seemed when she was little, is more fragile than I knew then. She's in her midthirties now and hanging on like that determined squirrel upside down on the birdfeeder. She comes down the back stairs and I know she's hoping no parents will be lurking in the kitchen. It's too much, this moving back home. Boundaries broken. Heart wide open and beating for all the world to see. My house is her house now, and her presence a reminder of so many layers of my life. It's a rebuke at times too, for things undone, hugs not given. Occasionally I get glimpses of new possibilities, a space in some future house with resentments laid to rest, like obstreperous children finally asleep in their cribs.

In her ferocious determination not to be depressed, I see that she has internalized all those early lessons and now has a few to teach me. Completely independently she has found a powerful spiritual life, gathered from the smooth stones of Buddhism, Christianity and other sources more dimly understood by me.

Sometimes we pray out loud together, a little self consciously, treading lightly for fear that in talking to God we might find ourselves unconsciously instructing each other.

Hannah is an artist, born with taste, high intuition, and an original approach to the world. When she was in nursery school her teacher said, "Hannah isn't very keen to do what all the other children are doing; she would prefer to create a new activity and entice them to join her." Not too long ago she had an artist's yard sale, cleaning out our attic and basement of her accumulated stuff. Along with the items to be sold is a long list of about seventy behaviors she would like to let go of, from yearning to live happily ever after to needing to have the last word. She turned the list into a long scroll and hung it on the fence where it could be carefully scrutinized by the shoppers.

I challenged her on a few items on the list. "Striving?" I said. "Why would you want to stop striving?"

"Well, it really means striving in meditation, the kind of striving that keeps you from being in the moment," she replied. Just as the first "early birds" were arriving she lost the stickers that were to be put on each object and thus matched numerically to the behavior list. For ten minutes we looked frantically for the plastic bag with the stickers but when the first customer had paid for his tea pot and lacrosse stick, Hannah gave up on the stickers and sent him to the scroll. "Pick a number," she said. "Maybe there's something on that list that you resonate with." A Haitian taxi driver bought an old stereo set and picked "worrying about being sick." One woman kept coming back for more things just so she could cross a few more behaviors off the list. All day new conversations bubbled along among strangers about behaviors that serve us and those that don't. I want to see a list of the behaviors she is left with, now that the black magic marker has struck out so many, but I don't dare ask.

Hannah was awarded an artist residency for the summer. Like moth to flame, she was drawn to the subject of the competition: homesteading. She was in the process of dehomesteading, having just broken up with her boyfriend and sealed her belongings in storage in a 12,000-cubic-foot pod. Her installation is to be a windsock of the same dimensions, perched on a hilltop field on Bumpkin Island in Boston Harbor, catching the breezes. Her title: EMPTY FULL, like lungs breathing, like the tides, like the cycles of our lives.

On a Friday morning I head out to the island to be part of her construction team. Our tiny ferry mows along through the glinting ocean, the wind whipping in big funnels around us. From the dock I walk the full circumference of the island looking for her and feeling the ghostliness of the place. These islands were places that people were hidden away: imprisoned, hospitalized, quarantined. Pequot Indians were interned on Long Island where famine, disease and the elements killed most of them. Boston's first real prisons were out here, on the theory that if you escaped you'd probably drown before you made it to the mainland. Orphanages and homes for delinquents were built out here and on Bumpkin there was a children's hospital, built in that yellow brick that reminds me of public institutions bent on saving money. As I walk along through the brush I see the piles of rubble it has become.

I am finally guided to Hannah's hilltop site by another artist and find a team putting together the structure that she has so carefully designed with her artist/engineer brain and her pauper's budget. It is made of PVC pipe and Ikea shower curtains in a soft pinky beige. Her helpers include rock climbers skilled in tying knots and stringing ropes. After half a day we are standing before a softly billowing structure, twice my height and three times my length. It is exactly the dimensions of all her possessions, which, aside from her car, are now in her storage pod and in her studio. It starts to rain and everyone on the island crams into our shimmering shelter.

She gets a stipend of $100. Artists live on the honor of residencies and commissions. She coaches artists too, which brings in some income, but like George, she is sometimes in a "pecuniary panic." She has been entirely self-supporting since she graduated from Brown fourteen years ago, but now, in the face of the country's deepest depression in many years, she has moved home.

We have concluded together that God arranged this. We've both got work to do, we think he's saying, in this business of loving. I sent her father away when she was five, interrupted her love, her childhood. We pass our pain through the generations. How do you break the chain?

At home, I tiptoe around her, fearing to say the wrong thing, so saying nothing.

I find this most remarkable letter that Erastus wrote to Nettie when she was 18.

Northampton, Sab Evg Oct 9th 1866

My dear sweet Daughter,

The day after I left you I was moved in spirit to write you a letter, but I did not. It was to have been the shortest, sweetest letter ever written. If you had received a sheet of this paper without date, address or signature with the single word

Darling

Written thus in the middle of it you would have had the embodiment of my conception. And now what more can I add. Does not that word express more in its solitude than with any adjectives? Consonants cannot unfold its meaning. They will only dictate its force. So take that word. Bury it deep in the warm soil of your virgin heart and let it germinate forth its full significance. It will grow and grow until it fills and thrills your entire being. Carry it with you through life and to the other life beyond the grave; through time and eternity let it speak to you of your

Father

It is almost scary, this letter. He writes so completely with his whole heart. It would be considered crossing a boundary to write such a letter today. But I love the wholeheartedness of it. Erastus is distilling the message: you are worthy. He wrote this after Caro's death, when all his children were alive in his heart, as he saw his own death approaching.

Linc has written to Hannah. I had told him she was working through a lot of things and he decided to write and "cheer her up," as he put it in his next letter to me.

XVI

The "tongues in trees, books in running brooks,
sermons in stones & good in everything"

I HAVE HAD A SPATE OF GOOD READING LATELY. In Italy, huddled by our propane stove in the kitchen of our villa in Ostuni, I read *The Housekeeper and the Professor*, by Yoko Ogawa. The story has the breathtaking spareness of Japanese culture at its finest. A housekeeper comes to work for an elderly mathematics professor whose memory, owing to an automobile accident, lasts only eighty minutes and then cycles to nothingness. He pins little notes on his suit to remind himself of important things, like "the woman who comes each morning is your housekeeper." But his mathematical brain is intact. The professor presents the housekeeper and her eleven year old son with little problems to solve, and to my astonishment I find myself fully engaged in the beauty of these mathematical revelations. An insight unfolds for me: for some God is in the infiniteness of infinity, in its beautiful absoluteness. Long before I found God in a church, I found him in nature. That he is in numbers for others suggests that what I have always thought of as rationalists have their own avenues into God that may be invisible to me.

What would Erastus think of this ever-expanding view of God? He found nature to be a vast metaphor for the spiritual world. Did Erastus know Ralph Waldo Emerson, who so expanded for the world the idea of where God could be found by anyone with an ear cocked or a heart open? They are both born in the first decade of the nineteenth century, they both begin their careers as ministers and both give up the ministry as young men. Each loses a beloved first wife and goes to Rome to heal. Erastus's daughter, Nettie, will marry Emerson's second cousin whom Erastus would have known very briefly before he died. Charlotte's diary, several years after Erastus's death, records, with a certain breathless tone, a visit from "Mr. Emerson." Massachusetts is a small, stewing sort of place in the nineteenth century, burbling up very original ideas.

Just as Nettie is meeting Professor B.K. Emerson, her future husband, George Eliot is publishing the first installment of *Middlemarch*, in *Harper's Magazine* in December, 1871. I like to imagine that she or Charlotte read it to Erastus in his last months, though he died too soon to hear the end. I begin reading it on the long train trip from Ostuni to Venice, needing a thorough distraction. It takes some retraining to read those long periodic sentences, but by chapter three I am thoroughly acclimated and absorbed in the world of Dorothea Brooke. Her marriage to Casaubon, the old man clutching his scholar's veneer, takes me back into my twenty-three year old mind, so unable to imagine how long life is, or what marriage will really be like, so trusting that somehow everything will be for the best. Nettie comes out of Charlotte's letters in this era like a character sighing with love for her own professor. Her father has raised her up to be the heaven bound Dorothea. Did she fear, as I do, that on her bad days she is more like the beautiful Rosamond Vincy, shallow and selfish? Erastus knew this vain female who lingers like a serpent in all women. When she was in Ipswich he wrote a little sermon to Nettie on vanity.

Northampton December 21 1862

My dear little Nettie,

...Little things are often very precious, and sometimes very brilliant. Goodness and intense beauty seems often to delight in concentration, and to pack the emotions away in the smallest

compass, as the pearl contains purity, the diamond brilliancy &
the opal gathers the choicest hues from the rays of light to flash
its tiny, gorgeous, changing darts upon the eye of the charmed
beholder. Well, what shall my " little Nettie" be? She should be
purer than the pearl, & more brilliant & charming than the
diamond or opal? In fact so superior to them that they should
become the mere aids and adjuncts of her beauty—like the
"ornaments about her neck." The ornament should never be
greater than the thing adorned. A woman can never... more
fully demonstrate her entire want of taste–than when she decks
herself in precious stones each of which are purer, more brilliant
& more beautiful than her own spirit...

How beautiful would be a royal court, if for every ray that
flashed from the gorgeous tiaras & bracelets & rings, a purer &
higher ray shot upward from the immortal spirit.
This letter will prove that I think of you and love you...
—Your affectionate Father

This letter comes to my mind one evening at an early music
concert in Jordan Hall in Boston. The audience is distinctly un-
adorned. They are an old variety of Bostonian, truly there for
the music, for the most part oblivious of their own appearance.
One sweet old lady has a Robin Hood-like orange hat with felt
jalapeno peppers growing out of it. Moths have been quietly
chewing on it for years. She peers out from under the brim, her
face alight with an expression of pure joy at the music. "How
beautiful would be a royal court, if for every ray that flashed from
the gorgeous tiaras & bracelets & rings, a purer & higher ray shot
upward from the immortal spirit." Suddenly it all comes together
for me; Erastus's little sermon to Nettie was the porridge of New
Englanders for generations. Now it simply goes without saying;
we hardly know why it is we are so uninterested in bling. Boston
is a city of modesty, and newcomers instinctively take up the
habits of filtered Calvinism.

I believe *Middlemarch* is the best book I have ever read in the English language for its extraordinary nuanced insight into human foibles and character. It seems the perfect companion to Erastus's letters, making visible that nineteenth century world in which they all lived, where life revolved around God and the coming of trains.

Now I am reading George's book and every paragraph gets my brain working as if it were lightning charging out to make new connections. I eat lunch with Peter and take him a few of George's morsels to chew on. Peter is an absolutist about quite a few things. "There are no shortcuts," he says. "Just hard work learning what you need to know." He drills down, in literature, music and art. For years I couldn't persuade him to look at Asian art; there was just simply too much he wanted to know about western art. Now he has become devoted to all things Japanese. A year ago he had never used a computer. He always had an assistant who did what needed to be done. He wrote in longhand with a Mirado Black Warrior Number Two pencil. But then he retired. Now he buys his Viennese opera tickets on line and follows Major League Baseball religiously through its website. But he is no fan of this technology. Too many shortcuts, too many temptations. He becomes more radical, more wary. I admire this in him, but I am drawn to hope, to finding good in what is.

A leading character in our lives is our son-in-law Andrew who lives a lot of his life on the internet. He is the web guru for a major New York publishing company and on the side has developed a delicious game that he is marketing through his extraordinary (to us) network. He has spent years developing and testing the game, playing hundreds of rounds with friends and friends of friends. He has named it Anomia, which means "the inability to name objects or to recognize the written or spoken names of objects."

Andrew has passion about all things in life: his music (he plays the saxophone, the guitar and the saw, and he composes); his family: Eamon at three, Margaret, one, and his wife, my daughter, Jody. And now his game, his new entrepreneurial passion. I see this as a return in some ways to the pre-industrial personality, to the kind of world Erastus knew. No longer can our children count on jobs for life. They need to have multiple pursuits, some that make money, some that might, but above all, some that feed the soul. Andrew, like Erastus, works mostly from home. He is present in the lives of his children. Much of this variety of pursuits is nurtured by the existence of the internet. He summons friends and community to his performances through Facebook and Twitter. He markets his game to a network of hundreds of friends who in turn have hundreds more friends reachable by pressing send. A woman in Australia reading a book about Alzheimer's that had the word Anomia in it searched for the meaning on Google and up came Andrew's game. She ordered it and played with her friends in Brisbane—and then emailed an offer to become the Australian distributor. Our children are in a fast moving current.

I never had a son and I find the affection of this man a thoroughly welcome addition to my life. He appears in our kitchen twice a week at about 9 a.m., with a child, or two, in tow with all their paraphernalia, and we have our brief and affectionate chats. Sometimes we find ourselves painting a room together or fixing a broken household item, and going to deeper places in our conversation. It is a relationship full of surprises and delicate mutual respectfulness. I am a little in awe of the gift I have suddenly been given here, of my new small family.

As Andrew was coming into our lives, Betty Davis, my stepmother of fifty years, was departing. She had had dementia for most of the decade since my father's death. She was well cared for and when I would visit she seemed to me happier than I had ever seen her in her life. She had reverted to a childlike state, taking wild pleasure in bright red autumn leaves, and forgetting all about the schemes and histrionics that had ruled her so long. Then she broke her hip at ninety-four and began her final departure. In the last few days her children and stepchildren and grandchildren slept in her hospital room, sang and talked to her absent self—everything from Buddhist meditations to the songs in harmony we'd sung as children washing the dishes. On the eighth day she died. It was April. The crab apple trees were in blossom and we picked a spot in the Arboretum we knew she would have loved. Andrew played the saxophone, sweetly mournful. We read things she loved, had chosen for others whose services she had organized. Just at the end my brother Jon who had chosen not to be in the program stood up, and bracing his feet one behind the other as he had since he was a little boy, slowly said, "I cannot let this end without saying one thing forever to her credit. She never stopped trying to learn to love." He sat back down and Andrew played "When the Saints Go Marching In."

Erastus's letters are about passing love and moral fiber on to his children. A message of drilling down, Peter's way, no shortcuts. I am contemplating how we can resume the generational transmission. Love was somehow interrupted in our family and we are having to learn it all over again. Erastus is a wonderful teacher.

I sometimes take Eamon to my black church, though Andrew is not keen on "religion." Eamon sits rapturously on my lap, listening to the music, catching the spirit. We say our "thank yous" together and sometimes puzzle over the shifting sands of relationships. "Oma, if Asa hits me is he my friend?" he asks me one day. Like the necklace handed down from one generation to another, we put our beads on this one together, one at a time.

My own father was almost entirely unable to express his emotions. What happened? How did the Victorian and Edwardian eras suck the passion and confidence out of three generations? They left children who were rigidly raised, valued for their accomplishments, like prized possessions, who were to be seen and not heard. Quite a few of them became adult narcissists, lacking in empathy. Sitting in a doctor's office this week, I read an article that says the very best predictor of adult happiness is an array of consistently loving people in a child's life. To be Oma everyday to Eamon and Margaret is the unexpected gift, a chance to be fully present for a new generation. Erastus understood the gift and how to express his enduring love. In his failing handwriting he wrote to Swint:

Home, Feb 25, 1869

My very dear son,

You have hardly got home, & I sit down to write to you—not a letter—but a little note of affection....

... I love you, my dear son, with an affection which you cannot comprehend, & my thoughts of love & intense solicitude brood, habitually, over you & your precious children...

Your father, Erastus Hopkins

I yearn to be able to say such things to my children.

Something new is happening in this generation. We have lived for twenty-five years in the same house, hardly knowing our neighbors. Now my children have come home to live in the area and suddenly I know everyone, and everyone knows me. I am Eamon's Oma, Jody and Hannah's Mom. The network is vast and its communication instantaneous. It's changing my own habits. I figured out that the Guatemalan who pumps my gas is named Willie and say "Hi Willie" one day. His eyes bug out of his head. He looked at my credit card and says "Anna, si?" We are in small town America.

I write another letter to Linc. I tell him about Hannah's yard sale and Andrew's game. I am trying to gently egg him on to do something useful in there, without sounding like a Victorian moralist. You are an accumulation of your experiences over a life-time, and it's scary to think of the experiences that accumulate in a decade of prison.

XVII

"We are here."

JULY HAS COME. WE ARE STILL WAITING FOR SUMMER. Every day of June has been blanketed in fog and rain. My spirits are in a liquid suspension. On impulse I decide to go alone to commune with the ancestors and play with my cousins. I will visit our family place in Maine to paint for a week and get away from my sadly waterlogged city garden.

I take the three-hour drive up the Maine Turnpike to Augusta. Then a right turn towards the coast. Penobscot Bay is really a series of fjords. If you were a gull, you would look down and see our point halfway between Castine and Blue Hill. But for land bound creatures it is a two-hour drive over the knuckles of a geological hand. Down the thumb, right out to the tip of the nail. The macadam turns to dirt and the impenetrable forests on either side of the road become a mossy fairy dell of grey lichened boulders and fir trees stretching their limbs contentedly. My cousin Sam's tender work of winter burning and spring planting, a magic forest warmed by shafts of afternoon sun. I stop in a clearing circled with birches and inhale the salty pungent smell of the fir forest and the cold blue ocean. The intensity of the smell is gone in a moment, as if my taste buds were taken by storm and knocked unconscious.

This point of land has come down to my generation from my grandparents. I share it with a rotation of seventy siblings and cousins, ranging in age from seventy-five to three weeks. It astonishes me to think that almost every one of them can count Erastus as a third, fourth or fifth great grandfather, though he is not on the family radar screen at all.

On this trip I am staying in the little hillside cottage that my grandparents built when my brother and I were born and they needed to retreat from our ruckus in the "Big House"—the one with Emily Dickinson's notes tucked in the rafters. Eight cottages have been built over the years at discreet distances from each other: plenty to house us all for a couple of weeks in the summer.

My grandfather, who found this land, was Erastus's grandson, Nettie's son. Erastus died three years before he was born, and I have only the evidence of his letters to tell me how much love he would have lavished on my Grandpa, Kendall. But somehow I think that love has found its way down to us anyway and is what lets us keep peace among seventy relatives who all think they own the place.

I have a letter Erastus wrote to little Sadie one summer about fifty years before grandfather came across this land. He too was on the coast of Maine, at Cape Elizabeth near Portland, and wrote:

> "*We are here. Where "here" is your Papa will show you on the map. There are two lighthouses on the point and they are both lighted at night to light up the Atlantic Ocean for 25 miles around, so that the sailors can see where the shore and rocks are. It must be a big lamp to light so large a space. The Ocean is all around us, & the roaring of the waves is heard all the time, day & night. There is a beach, where we often wish you were with us to pick up shells. Mamama & Aunt Nettie went in bathing right out in the Ocean & Aunt Sadie went with me, & we walked to the lighthouses... We are just going to church about three quarters of a mile off. I think I see you trotting along with your Papa. Goodbye my darling, We speak of you often & we are all full of love to you, Your affectionate, Dante*"

Erastus took his family on many summer trips and particularly loved the Adirondacks, but the concept of a "summer place" was a generation or two down the road. Somewhat mysteriously there is a mountain named for Erastus in the Adirondacks. I like to imagine that his travels there had something to do with the Underground Railroad, though I have no concrete evidence of this. It was an area that fugitives both travelled through on their way to Canada, and settled in. John Brown's farm and burial place is there. According to the ADK High Peaks region guidebook, it was Erastus (Rev. Hopkins) who suggested to the mountain guide Old Mountain Phelps the name "Resagone" (The King's Great Saw) for the high peak now known as Sawteeth. If Old Man Phelps did the naming of the peaks, perhaps he named Hopkins Mountain as a tribute to a friend. In the fall of 2008 I climbed to the summit with an old schoolmate, a skilled climber. I hadn't climbed a mountain in decades and had had knee surgery a few months before, but for eight hours, up and down, some kind of warm mystical energy moved me forward through the Mossy Cascade up to the top. I was like Sadie, trotting along beside "Dante." The summit is a great granite ledge, a tilted saucer. We peeled oranges and chocolate bars and lay down on a mossy bit, listening to the bees at their eternal work. "Sawteeth," in a swirl of red and yellow foliage, watched us impassively across the valley.

I have something of the same moment of union with my grandpa when I arrive at the low cliff at the end of the thumbnail, looking out at Pumpkin Island Light across from Little Deer Isle. Grandpa first saw it from the sea in 1910 cruising with his friends. He was thirty-five. The First World War was about to begin, but Americans would not be drawn in for a while yet. By 1918 he would be working with the American Red Cross on an expedition in Siberia, but for now he had the extraordinary opportunity to buy a whole peninsula of the Maine Coast with his two best friends. They bought several hundred acres from the Cape Rosier Land Corporation for $10,000. It had been on the market since 1863. In my father's cheerful accounting, the land was a place to park the women and children while the men went sailing.

The land had at some point been clear-cut for lumber and there were no roads in, which may have been why it was on the market for fifty years. The three men built their houses from materials brought by barge, and lived in the meantime with their families in big tents. Even today we can divide the family into would-be tent dwellers and those who like their comforts and their internet connections. For the most part, I am a tent dweller, but in this six weeks of rain, I would have surely gone over to the other side.

If you look at photographs of old summer houses on the Maine coast, you will see a lot of sturdy, handsome wicker furniture: couches, end tables, armchairs. It was all bought from the Sears and Roebuck Catalogue of the time and is indestructible. These pieces could easily last another several generations, if a lust for newness does not intervene. Since these domestic furnishings bought in the second decade of the twentieth century have only been used for two months of every year, those which started out with my grandmother (ca. 1920) are really only about fifteen years old in "use time."

A gravel path up through the woods leads to the chapel, Our Lady of the Evergreens. What thoughts and discussions led to its creation? Perhaps they knew that there would be serpents lurking in this Eden of our family and considered that creating a shared spiritual tradition might ward them off? The chapel is a consecrated church in the Episcopal Diocese of Maine. Anyone can come any Sunday in the summer, park at the top of the hill and walk three minutes through the woods. The building is a simple two-by-four construction in the shape of a cross that seats roughly fifty people and has a vestry and a short bell tower. Bell ringing is a coveted chore of the ten and unders, as lighting and extinguishing the candles is for the teenagers. The warning bell sounds promptly at 9:50 every Sunday of the summer and in whatever state of morning stupor I am in, I always feel the same little tremor in my gut at the sound. I am summoned, not by the child ringing the bell, but by my grandmother who's been dead for forty years.

At the second bell the family slides into their usual spots among the visitors. Dogs meander up the aisles and infants crawl around and fuss. Even chaos has its sanctity. It is the only church I know where the congregation looks out a large window as they worship, at the moving hand of God. The view is the Atlantic Ocean, different every Sunday, with Eagle Island and Little Deer off in the distance. Or maybe just fog and a hint of fir trees.

My uncle, Sewall Emerson, and his friend, Jack Hawkins, performed the service for forty years or so, one in July and the other in August. Various family members and neighbors read the lessons, take the offering, and pump the organ. Sometimes we are graced with a musically talented visitor and have a mini concert as part of the service. A couple of old log books in the vestry (also used as the internet hot spot during the week) faithfully describe every service since the beginning: Sundays, weddings, baptisms, memorial services. They include any special people who were there, the number in attendance, who officiated and how much the collection came to. Every service ends with "Eternal Father Strong to Save" (the Navy Hymn), "America the Beautiful," and my grandmother's favorite prayer [see note]. Communion is given every Sunday and the rules are informal: so informal that my daughter Jody, at three, called to her cousin from the Communion rail, "Grace, don't you want to have snack?"

When Uncle Sewall died, Perry Williams, the retired Bishop of Cleveland, took over the service. Now he is gone too, and we are holding our collective breath, hoping that Linc's sister Grace, that Erastus lookalike, now a student at the Episcopal Divinity School, will soon take on the role.

Up in my aerie of a screen porch on the hill I watch the light creep across the cockeyed roofs of the "Big House" below me, turning them from silver to grey to gold. Eight boys and one girl are playing a boisterous game of hide and seek. I can hear them in their hiding places whispering to each other. I'm invisible, taking in who's the boss, who's shy, who's clever, who's generous to the little ones. Watching them is like having an oxygen canister of childish glee pump through this wheezing old soul of mine. I am all the children and all the ancestors at once.

Looking around this little cabin of my grandparents I marvel at the simplicity with which they lived. Every year for at least two months they slept and ate and dressed in this one little room, tidying up their beds in the morning so they looked like couches, pulling the curtains, I suppose, to dress. Now there is a little back bedroom where I sleep, built for their caretaker when my grandparents were in their eighties. I love this pared down life, so elusive in this time of plenty.

The cabin looks like a railway car with a mini kitchen caboose. This year I am sharing it with a very bold chipmunk who likes gingersnaps. The square little kitchen still has Grandma's Dundee Marmalade jars on a shelf holding the silverware, and the same yellow linoleum countertop with little gold specks, with an aluminum rim that works nicely for opening beer bottles. Just walking into it is like looking into a funhouse mirror of my life, reverberating those moments of joy, shame, empty desperation and total completion. Whatever my emotional state, here it is distilled.

From the small screened front porch my Grandfather used to hold forth with his megaphone, directing traffic on the float a hundred yards below him or telling us how to tie a bowline (the rabbit comes up out of the hole, goes around the tree and down the hole again). The summer I was twelve it was my turn in the rotation of female cousins to "look after" my grandparents who were then in their eighties. I cooked them eggs and toast and made them little salads for lunch, taking in their wisdom on the use of salt and the fluffing of pillows. We would eat looking out at their little garden, which now has an eight-foot cedar tree growing in it.

Grandpa, a lifelong smoker, ironically was also the longtime director of the National Tuberculosis Society. At eighty-five he had a rasping kind of bark and held his cigarette tenderly between his nicotine stained fingers. He was a little scary, a firm believer that children should be "seen and not heard." Now I can see his life in a clearer frame: the little boy who was the object of Emily Dickinson's ethereal affection at one end, and the old man with his watery blue eyes and parchment skin waiting on the Lord, at the other. The generations just tumble and heave, like glaciers sped up, raking across our lives, heedlessly depositing in us their best, and their worst.

Of all my siblings and cousins, my brother and I are the ones most possessed of a desire to keep the weird trophies of our ancestors, to maintain the museum. I put on a starchly ironed apron with a faded red cherry pattern (really only fifteen years old after all) and I instantly feel my grandmother's presence light the room. The eggbeater with the green wooden handle is practically new: she brought it here in 1920. Then there are the real trophies, the racing flags tacked up around the living room to celebrate a sailing victory of my parents, and some unnamed ancestor's bridge trophies.

Digging through photographs I find some early ones: of the huge tents they lived in while they were building the houses, of a clambake on the beach, cooking layers of clams and lobsters in barrels of seaweed. Tonight we cooked lobsters in giant aluminum pots on the rocks. Everyone brought something. Seventeen of us.

In my mind this cottage holds my grandparents still, end to end, in their narrow single beds on their white bedspreads with red and blue sailboats on them. Grandpa died the year after I took care of them and Grandma lived another decade, some of it in a fury that she was still alive. One of those summers she launched down the gravel path in the pitch dark and hurled several pounds of sirloin steak into Penobscot Bay. Days later she was in McLean Hospital. I was fourteen and either I knew better than to ask questions or I asked, and got no answers.

It takes days to allow myself to sink gently into the nighttime silence here. At first I fight it. I turn on the radio, listen to my book on tape started on the road trip. The silence is so complete, it empties me, and makes me feel a little scared, like I might fall into Alice's rabbit hole, or my Grandmother's steak-pitching darkness. My usual antidote to silence is Peter, always to be counted on for stimulating conversation. But this is not his kind of place. He likes cities, performances, things to do and see that are happening right now. It torments me, and it doesn't.

Mark and Ruthie are right up the hill in the new house they've just built. Noah, Linc's son, is with them. He has been in their care since Linc went to prison and they have finally won their battle in court to get full custody of him. He is now a handsome fourteen-year-old with a passion for music. He plays an electric guitar on any stage he can find. He has reddish blond hair, blue eyes and a kind of racing spirit that reminds me of his grandfather. He is a boy in America with all the distractions and temptations that are likely to lead him away from Erastus's "piety, temperance and diligence," but he is in the heart of a big family that has more than the usual measure of those things.

As I sit inside my screen porch reading one afternoon, Noah comes down the hill looking out of sorts and plops himself down in a mossy little patch right across the path from my house. He lies there on his back for ten minutes or so and I wonder if he knows that I am sitting twenty feet away or whether he is just in his own world. I feel as if we are two soap bubbles, floating with their rainbows in the afternoon sun, and that if we collide we will both just go poof and vanish. Such is the tentative nature of this yearning relationship I have with him. I want him to feel himself in this powerful web of familial love that stretches back centuries in time. But I fear he might go poof in the way that adolescents sometimes do. Come to think of it, my grandmother probably had something of the same yearning, to fill me with good things, to make up somehow for the mother I had lost, that I have for Noah.

XVIII

The sky has not fallen yet, & so I
have caught no stars for you…

W E HOLD ALL OUR EARLIER SELVES somewhere inside, like a Russian doll, down to the littlest being, and for me in this place they come popping out. I suddenly remember a pink flowered bathing suit with a little skirt I wore when I was six, and my mother sitting on the porch smoking a cigarette. Is it a dream or a photograph? Do I really hold that memory inside? What does Noah's littlest doll remember?

Since I arrived we have had two days of sun; then more rain. On sunny days I am in a stream of adolescents who flow by my little cottage window, letting breezy little whisps of conversation drift in the window. Noah is in love with a girl from Paris. One day I notice that when I slam the refrigerator door it makes the radio go on and I invite a pair of young cousins to come in and hypothesize with me why this might be. The puzzle remains unsolved, but we add a little stitch together in the family fabric.

My eleven-year-old cousin (once removed) Alex comes by with his newspaper, the *Dog Island Point News*, with the headline: "Young Film Crew Storms Point." This is his third summer as the Point reporter, editor and publisher and we all rush to read the latest news of the pre-pubescent. It is unabashedly frank and delicious. Each issue has an interview with a cousin, this one with his brother Nicholas, known as Pickle, on the subject of pickles and how he relates to them. (He hates them.) Alex has a side business collecting all of our recyclables and will surely be a scientist or an engineer.

On rainy days there is a steady patter on the roof. No children's footsteps passing by. I work on a painting I started in the sunlight. It is of the guesthouse, a brown and green structure with two curtained windows at the end winking like eyes. Not the most beautiful thing I could paint, but at least I can sit in front of it, not too far from my hillside cottage. So if I've forgotten something (like bug spray), the recovery is not insurmountable. When I started there were lots of shadows playing in the light, but today all is washed in gloom. I spend the first couple of hours contemplating the mass of muddy green I've created, with several books on painting in my lap. I map out a strategy involving much more careful color mixing: lightening the whole thing up, and waiting for nature to bring back the sunlight.

Why am I so driven to paint? I know that the way to get good at this is to suspend my understanding of the object I am painting. Squint at it and see it as slashes of light and dark. Make something pleasing of those patterns in colors that work together. It is hard to do: the superficial "reality" of the subject keeps demanding my attention. In truth I am driven to paint things I know and love, as if I want to immortalize them and hold them close forever. But in painting them I must let go of them as mere objects and places. I must find their spirit.

I am reading in this moment Thomas Merton's *The Seven Story Mountain*, am charmed by the ways he paints his early life in words, with great big brushstrokes of what he sees and feels, as if he has no internal censorious voice muttering at him.

While I wait out the rain and listen to its quiet pattering on the roof, I think about Gabriel, my six-year-old nephew whom I invited yesterday to have an adventure with me. Of the choices offered (picking mussels, building a fort or painting a picture), he leapt at the painting option.

"A bowl of fruit," he suggested with no breath drawn. On the exhale, he mused about pears, maybe a bunch of grapes, and yes, bananas, "we've got to have bananas." So all of these I acquire in my afternoon's shopping. Gabriel appears in his red slicker and settles down to paint. The result is an exquisite piece of disconnected oozing spidery color, clearly recognizable as individual pieces of fruit, and in its creation, a little opening for us to be friends.

Gabriel was born weighing under a pound and a half, to my youngest brother and his wife. He was in his incubator for about three months, like a very alert little bird: wary. Except at large gatherings, I have rarely seen this little nephew, and it is only this unplanned trip to Maine that has offered the opportunity. So our painting encounter is (for me) freighted with a desire to please and to establish some ground for a future relationship. This is a place of geology and generations, of natural cycles, of the old teaching the young. Erastus was never here but he's part of this circle, an earlier ripple in this pond. This place challenges that linear theology we live by in our other life: our steadfast belief in the rightness of progress.

Eventually the sun comes out and I go back to my spot by the guesthouse. I have a strategy now: forget what color it really is. Find a color that's pleasing. Create a palette that works. I set myself up and work long after the light has changed too much. Children come and go and look over my shoulder.

"What's that pink thing?" asks Chance.

"A rock," I answer. A bit later he comes back.

"Does it look more like a rock now? I've been working on it."

Chance is going into fourth grade in Hong Kong and is offering lessons in Mandarin to anyone on the point who will pay him fifty cents an hour. He is doing quite well in this enterprise.

I have three oil paintings in various stages of completion after six days. I am smitten with the early evening and can hardly walk outside without wanting to paint the big strokes of light that are falling on the upper branches of the fir trees. When the darkness comes I pick up my book and each of the letters leaps up at me, wriggling around in little frocks of color, as if they're crying "paint me." Vertical and horizontal lines of type turn into splashing green branches of fir, and violet roof lines. Then the words, conjuring Merton's farmhouse in the Auvergne in the snow, start turning into slashes of whiteblue, shimmering paint on the page. Time to go to bed.

Each day I've had another moment with Noah. One evening while I am cooking dinner, he pauses on his way by my cottage. The track between his house fifty feet up the road and the house where his favorite cousins are staying runs right below my porch. He hangs from the railing below me, and like a kid on a jungle gym chins himself, leaps up on to the porch and down again, and asks me questions. He's tall, almost five foot ten, and handsome with reddish gold curls, like his grandmother Ruthie and her great grandmother, my Nettie. He has the thirsty energy of a fourteen year old, looking for new springs of activity and challenge.

"So I hear you write to Linc, Aunt Anne." Ruthie had told me that he had decided one day that he would no longer call Linc his Dad, just Linc, as if he were holding him out at arms length for examination. We talk in the dusk until the mosquitoes come out, about Linc, our letters and visits, about what Noah hopes for when he gets out.

Another day he drops into my front porch and asks me about my stepmother. "I hear Betty was pretty crazy," he said. "What was it like to grow up with that?" So I tell him all about her.

I walk up to Ruthie's one morning and find Noah wrapped around his guitar, practicing Leonard Cohen's "Hallelujah," for a Sunday morning performance in the chapel. It's hard to say which is more important to him right now: wine, women or song. But women and wine are hard to come by at fourteen, so song is his consuming passion. In the line of cousins he is the second oldest. There are more than twenty of them in his generation who rotate through here in the summer, each one a little twig of Erastus's tree.

A letter comes one day from Linc. He describes his cell in the Max II unit "on a status called ITS" which I take to mean Intensive Treatment Status. He stays on "a locked corridor with my cell door open or room door open and the steel metal grill door at the end of the corridor locked so I have the whole hallway to pace up and down on or run back and forth in its about 50 yards long or so. When one of the guys on the unit needs to get into his room they just shut my door and lock it then open up the steel ITS door." This is his reality now and he finds little daily pleasures in it, like having his cell door open. I wonder if he ever closes his eyes and takes himself here, into the sparkling sunlight of the Bay.

My cousin Betsy has asked me to prepare the chapel for the Sunday service. I am to unlock the silver chalice, get some good bread for communion, and put flowers in the vases at the bay window. I am to assign the readings to members of the family, and give the children their tasks in the service. And to sweep out any pinecones brought in by the winter residents during the week. I bring Eamon with me for the cleanup while Margaret sleeps in her crib thirty feet down the hill.

Eamon has been watching the big boys making wooden swords and guns in the woodshop with great interest. We have all given up trying to make pacifists out of these children and have fallen back on the idea that as long as the play is imaginative, pretend violence is tolerable.

"Oma, do you need to be killed?" Eamon asks me solicitously, pointing an empty squirt gun at me. He has been making this offer to all of us for days. We vary our answers to give him an opportunity to work this life and death thing out.

"This is my alive gun," he says if we have submitted to being killed. "Now you're alive again," and "pop, bop" he goes.

We sit together on a bench in the chapel, just the two of us, and look out at the Bay, the clouds slipping across the window like the little lambs in his sister's farm book. We are in the stream together, with Aunt Esther and Erastus, Nettie and Josephine, my mother and father. For a brief second I see this little grandson, not as three and three-quarters, but as twenty and thirty and seventy. Across the room he spies Noah's Ark with all its little animals, two by two, and hops off to play. The alive gun sits on the bench beside me.

The summer wanes and the Point reverts to its natural still-ness. I get up alone one indigo blue morning and drink my coffee on the porch looking over the dancing diamond facets of the Bay. There seems to be a convention of birds I've never seen before. They are tiny, and dart and swoop in trios, flashes of yellow and orange, crying a high pitched see, see, see. They are like the chil-dren of summer in their unabashed sociability. I think they must be the Golden Kinglets that Hannah had watched learning to fly in July. I hear a tiny hummingbird hovering around the feeder and I turn, very slowly, so as not to startle him. He tries each of the four spigots and then checks to make sure he hasn't missed one at the top. I am like a small seashell washing in the waves, perfectly empty.

I drive into Blue Hill in the fog and pick up a *Boston Globe*. On the front page is a picture of the Middlesex County Jail, Linc's Jail, in revolt. It is being closed down because some prisoners have bashed in the sprinkler system on three floors, in a coordinated act of boredom and spite. It's like the slash of a dragon's tail into our peaceful woods.

A few days later, Linc's mother Ruthie, my favorite, dear cousin, arrives. She tells me that Linc was transferred with all the other prisoners for a day or so to another prison, but is now back in his familiar territory. The sprinkler orgy was orchestrated by some guys on the floor below. We look at each other with relief. It would have been Linc last year, but now, we say to each other, he's learned his lesson.

After the last chapel service of the summer I pack up my wet paintings (three in all) and stuff of daily living and head back to Boston. The drive gets longer every year, and not just because I am older. There is development everywhere and I imagine that my great grandchildren will have a hard time finding the solitude

I have just enjoyed for this week. Peter has been to the Montreal Jazz Festival in this period of time and we arrive almost simultaneously in a state of exhaustion from our many road miles.

A day or two later I.go to visit Linc. I've got every piece of the drill down now. An efficient call to Desiree to get the green light. Quarters in hand for the parking meter and the locker for my belongings. I even go up in the elevator without an escort. The rules change a little according to the whim of whoever is in charge at the moment. I go into the visitor room, this time taking in the cute antique red screen door that slides electronically to lock me into the visitors' space. Kind of homey, like you're in grandma's kitchen, but I realize for the first time that I am being locked in. I have come to this visit in a very different state of mind than two months ago when I was full of trepidation. Now I'm just here.

I sit there for ten minutes and Linc finally arrives. Just as he enters, one of the COs, as he calls them, says something complimentary to him, which I can't quite hear. I store the moment away to ask him about. He is looking much more relaxed than the last time, but radiating a strange energy. He reminds me of what I feel like when I have done a forty-five minute biking class at my gym. Endorphins rising.

He says he's sorry I had to wait a few minutes and explains in a circuitous way that he had not gotten up yet. It's eleven thirty in the morning.

"You look good, more relaxed than the last time I saw you."

"Yeah, I'm definitely feeling better."

So, I hear you've had some excitement around here lately."

And he's off, telling me the whole saga. First there was a swine flu outbreak in the prison which resulted in some rearranging of prisoners. Linc was moved into a cell in the next unit over, the Isolation Unit, or "iso" as he calls it, where they keep the child molesters and rapists—those folks who would not fare well if left to fend for themselves in the general prison population.

"It's great in there, Aunt Anne. I have my own little anteroom in front of my cell, which is a lot better than just having your cell face directly out on the corridor. In my old cell I had to put up with prisoners walking up and down the hall as I was trying to read. That's what they do with iso prisoners: they make them walk up and down in the corridor for exercise, they can't go to the basketball court or anything. And on the Fourth of July I got to watch the fireworks. It was fantastic. I bet I had the best view in the city."

But some of the prisoners were so freaked out by the swine flu that they bashed in the sprinkler system on the floor below him, figuring one way or another they would get out of the prison and away from the flu. Linc described how a guard came to his cell and said they had a "situation" and were going to have to move him. He cooperated fully. The CO that I had overheard was complimenting him because he didn't pull any funny stuff.

"They didn't have enough handcuffs so they put plastic ties on me, and me and two other prisoners from iso went in a mobile van, with squad cars in front and back, sirens blaring, all the way to Billerica. I spent five days there, wearing boxer shorts and a green wraparound "turtle suit."

"It wasn't so bad because I got to see some guys I know from when I was there before, and some COs I like. But it really freaked me out at first because that's where I really didn't have any privileges, no rec, no canteen. For exercise I had to walk up and down the corridor in a tether. That's when they put a rope between your ankle cuffs and handcuffs so you can't yank your hands up suddenly."

He tells me all this very matter-of-factly. This is his world. He likes his new "iso" cell so much he's petitioning the prison to keep him in there next to all the child molesters and rapists. They have better gym hours too and that's a big deal to him. He recently shot fifteen hoops in a row three times. We joke about his future career with the Celtics.

XIX

Witness

ERASTUS'S PORTRAIT HAS BEEN IN THE HANDS of a restorer since April and it's now September. I have called him a couple of times and he is reassuring, but always asks for a little more time. I do not have high hopes for this venture but I am quite willing to be patient because he is the only restorer I can afford. He is charging one tenth the price of all the other professionals in this field I have talked with. Norman Boas recommended him to me and his comment on the price was simple: "painting restorers are just like everybody else, they've gotten greedy and think they can get away with it."

We set a date to meet in two weeks. The restorer is in Connecticut but offers to split the drive with me and meet in Providence. We agree on the lobby of the RISD Museum at 11 am. I love this little museum and pick this spot so I can visit a couple of paintings I am especially fond of before he arrives. When the day comes, I am nervous. All the expensive restorers have filled me with trepidation about how the portrait will surely be thoroughly ruined if I don't sign up for their superior skill. I remind myself that the portrait was pretty thoroughly ruined before, with a big U-shaped rip from ear to ear and running right through the beard. A century and a half of grime obscuring whatever grace might have been in the original. But I am nervous nonetheless.

I arrive early. The museum is snugly nestled into College Hill, its older part blending into the brick facades of Benefit Street and the new wing visible as a little gleaming modern glass tower rising on Main Street below. The two sections are cleverly linked by small galleries snaking up the hill and I wind my way to my favorite pictures. My first stop is the Cy Twombly that looks like scribblings on a grey chalk board. It makes the hair on the back of my neck stand up just like fingernails running on the real item. Then I search out Manet's *Girl in a White Dress* sitting on a sumptuous tufted maroon velvet couch, looking so innocent and so seductive. How can an artist make paint do that? Is that burnt carmine that makes those tufts so erotic? When I come back to the lobby the restorer is sitting at the only table with the painting of Erastus leaning on the wall beside him, his nineteenth century presence a stark contrast to this modern white lobby. Erastus is looking out at me with an almost beating heart. He has been restored to beaming health. His ruddy face is stern and now I can clearly see his arms folded across his chest. This is Erastus the public man, the man of stature and of history. But I see him with Nettie's eyes, and hear that tender, passionate father's voice. I congratulate the restorer on his masterful work. He smiles modestly. James Harvey Young, the artist from Salem, would be pleased. I had been cautioned against the portrait being "over restored," tarted up by too much brightening, but what I see before me has all the subtlety of a great portrait, the nuances of character emerging as the light on the portrait changes.

I carry him carefully back to my car a block down the street and rest him in the back seat. He's looking a lot better than the last time he took this ride. I have been struggling with where to put the portrait in our house. My grandmother and my great grandfather are already very present in the dining room and living room. My "family things" are one of the hot buttons in our marriage and I think the warning lights are flashing. So perhaps Erastus can hang over my bed and greet me each morning. Right now I have an attentive angel from a Lorenzo Lotto painting in the spot he might occupy. Erastus has become a more personal, attentive angel, so Lorenzo Lotto's will have to make way.

Peter and I have planned a trip to New Mexico, a place that we have visited many times. We have timed it so that we can go to the Saint Geronimo Festival at Taos Pueblo on September 29 and visit Georgia O'Keefe's House and the Ghost Ranch in Abiqui. When I was twelve years old I bought a turquoise ring from a Zuni Indian at another festival at the Taos Pueblo and now I am bringing it back to New Mexico to be repaired. It's been on my right hand for fifty years and one of the prongs that holds the turquoise in place is lifting. The ring is an old thing now and the oil from my skin has turned the stones dark. Even repaired it will not have the sparkle of the bright new turquoise that's being sold at the San Geronimo Festival. I am tempted to buy a beautiful, heavy new ring, another Zuni creation, and I weigh the idea for a day while my old ring is repaired by "Bear," an old cowboy whose business is called "Guns for Hire." When I put the old ring back on my finger my decision is clear. The ring is old, but so is my hand and they go together. We have become intimate and it now is one of the few objects close enough to me to tell my story. My children have already started to mumble about who will get this symbol of me when I die. Maybe in a couple of hundred years this ring will be the artifact that sparks someone to resurrect my life. It qualifies.

The New Mexican landscape has a kind of radiant personality, maybe because every five or six miles the climate and vegetation changes. Sometimes it just whispers to you with tumbling sage brush. Then you turn a corner and a great mesa sheers up in front of you, brilliant red and yellow curves like a woman's breasts. Georgia O'Keeffe put it down in paint.

Travelling along in this landscape is like having a third person in the car making hilarious jokes and belting out old cowboy ballads. It just lifts your spirits and makes you open to the grace of other things that might happen along the way.

One of those moments came after dinner in a restaurant in Sante Fe. It was a new restaurant and a review hanging in the window caught my eye. The owner was a man about our age and watching him hover solicitously over his customers I wondered at his energy to begin such a demanding enterprise at this stage in life. Peter was in a sudden gloom, something I notice is happening more in these days of retirement, the forgotton-but-not-gone syndrome.

The owner of the restaurant is a large pear shaped man with black and white striped pants and a white chef's coat, and at the end of the meal he comes over to us and stands somewhat awkwardly at our table. I ask him what he did before this. He tells us he was the bass player in the Chicago Symphony for twenty years, under Solti and Guilini.

He grimaces as he says Solti's name. "What a prima donna." He is relaxing now, something about his eyes is changing, like he's seeing something that is not visible to me.

"Guilini was something else entirely. Such a sweet man. The orchestra loved him, and that doesn't happen so often," he laughed. "The Chicago Symphony was half Poles, half Slovaks, and they didn't get along at all. Always fighting. But for Guilini they calmed down. He was all about the silences between the notes. I never knew a conductor who could make you feel them like that. For him they played like a dream."

Peter is sitting back in his chair, resting his chin in his hand. I look over at him wondering how he is going to respond. He looks so handsome to me in that moment, kind of like an old conductor himself, with his tan, bald head and wild white fringe that I have been cutting for thirty years. Tenderness, in all of its meanings, is the word that comes to mind for that moment, mine for him and his in the world.

"Where were you before Chicago?" I ask.

"The Minnesota Orchestra. I landed a job there when I was twenty."

I look over at Peter.

"Are you going to tell him? " I ask. He shakes his head almost imperceptibly.

"Tell me what?" the owner asks.

"That he was the music critic on the Minneapolis Star when you were playing in the orchestra," I say, thinking that maybe I am going to hear about this betrayal of privacy later.

"What's your name?" They both ask at the same moment.

"Robert Chickering, like the piano company in Boston," our host replies.

The mood shifts to the shared intimacy of old friends. Thirty-five years after the fact they are sharing crystal clear moments, literally a few seconds, of a piece of music being played in a way they understood it would never be played again. They swap orchestra travel stories. Peter remembers the time he was covering the orchestra in New York and the airline had to put on a second aircraft to honor its promise to fly all ticketholders. So Peter flew alone, sitting opposite a solitary bass that had its own ticket.

"That could have been my bass," Chickering laughs. "It racked up a lot of miles. I always bought it its own ticket. A Midwest orchestra does a lot of flying to God-forsaken places in the frigid north, like Saskatoon."

"Or Fargo, North Dakota. I had some bleak nights there," says Peter. "We were probably on lots of the same flights." I listen to all of this sitting perfectly still. It is like watching a beautiful weather front sweep across the horizon pushing a murky smog out of the way. Each of them is a witness to the other, that these things had really happened, and mattered; that these are the funny and awesome moments which constitute a life. I am touched that two people could have so many common memories without ever having known each other, and that they can come upon each other in this unlikely circumstance. A retired theatre director and music critic, and a restaurant entrepreneur with a distinguished musical past, each thinking a little sadly that no one really knows who they have been in their lives.

We sit in the dim glow of the restaurant long after the last waiter had gone home, and finally, reluctantly, part.

"Santa Fe's a place where everyone has a story," Peter says when we are in the car. "It's a magnet for energetic talented people." I am sitting in silent awe at the exquisite timing of that moment of grace, and for once, I hold my tongue.

Back in Boston, it's time to visit Linc again. I have promised him I will try to come every month. I am a little nervous about what I will find because his father has told me that they are worried that he has been "cheeking" his medication—meaning hiding it in his mouth until the guard has departed and then spitting it out. This they have concluded because he did not seem well on their last visit.

The guards seem to recognize me this time and I go through to the visitors room, taking off my hair clip to get through the metal detector. I wait for a bit on my two plastic green chairs, and finally Linc appears. His prison uniform is baggy, a grey green. He still has the wide-eyed look of boy to me, but his very short buzz cut is going grey. He's a handsome guy, a little gaunt and his eyes move around the room rapidly. He's checking out who's in the guard booth behind me. I'm glad it's not the female guard who was on duty the last time. He greets me through the glass with a wave and a smile and then turns back to the guard to negotiate the removal of his handcuffs and leg irons. The guard takes them off, kneeling at his feet and I think to myself, that must not be a comfortable place to be.

When he picks up the telephone I am pleasantly surprised at how alert he is. He's not yawning. And he's full of stories to tell me. He describes an exercise routine which would put Marines to shame. He does five sets of one hundred push ups to start. Pull ups, sit ups, running in place. His routine consumes hours in his day. He is a man of iron and proud of it. All this with nothing but a deconstructed jail cell redesigned in his mind as a gym. Looking at him I can see that he is telling me something close to the truth, because the muscle definition in his neck, which is all I can really see, is startling. I can feel the energy driving him in the way he is talking, that no-breath-drawn rush that I could hear in his first letter to me.

He tells me that they've changed his medication and a lot of the side effects have gone away. I remember that his father said he hated the meds he was on because they kill his libido. I ask him if he misses his embezzler friend who was next door in his old cell.

"Well I've got an interesting guy next to me now, and I'm spending a lot of time advising him. He's only twenty-one and he's in here for having sex with a thirteen year old girl." He tells me all about his family from small town Massachusetts, and I can see how this kind of thing can happen in a place where kids don't have much to do. I imagine an innocent wide-eyed blond kid stunned at the misfortune of being accused of a felony when they were just having fun. Now he's really not having fun. And Linc is his protector?

"It was consensual, but it's still against the law. I think he's really got a raw deal. I'm kind of like playing a parent role with him, you know? I keep telling him that he's got his whole life ahead of him and that he's got to stay clean in here. He's already messed up a couple of times. Got caught masturbating in the shower and that's against the rules. I'm telling him how to take care of himself in here. This is not a nice place for sex offenders and especially if word gets around that they are doing things like that."

He's talking really fast—as in fast-talking me. Is he really trying to keep this kid on the straight and narrow, or is something else going on here? The reason he likes iso is that his cell is more private; it's got a little anteroom so everyone who walks by can't see in. He uses the word parental describing his relationship with his neighbor over and over, a little like a used car salesman. I realize I don't really want to know the truth. I am curious about this world, but I don't want to get sucked into it. It is a delicate balance. This is his life and he wants me to be here, but there are limits to the "here" I am willing to go to. He does not want to be alone. I offer him a prayer and he says "Sure." His eyes look empty. It doesn't flow as smoothly this time.

This will be the last visit for many months. Soon afterward he is moved to Bridgewater and for the next six months he is moved two or three more times, like a hot potato, between Middlesex and Bridgewater. His letters stop. He has stopped his medication.

He is put in serious isolation and forbidden visitors. I realize now that the last time I saw him he really had been cheating on this medication. His father recognized the symptoms long before I could have. To me he just seemed less sleepy, but that's the first sign, says his mother. While his father and his lawyer were meeting with him, he jumped a guard. He described the feelings to me last summer: a dark voice in his brain takes over like a relentless Pacman.

"It's like I'm playing a game and the point is to take advantage of every opening, find the enemy's weakness and seize upon it."

I think back on my visit with this new information and realize that it was this dark place that I was resisting going to with him.

I write him a letter. I enclose Erastus's love letter to Sarah. His sad, sad feeling at being apart from his son.

I take Erastus's portrait to be framed. I pick a simple black frame with a couple of muted gold stripes that echo the striped wallpaper behind him. The woman who is doing the job tells me that she has never handled a portrait quite like this.

XX

Tying My Shoes

I

T'S FALL. I PULL UP THE SHADE THIS MORNING to three golden
pear trees standing like sentries outside my window. Their
glow flows like a river into me, powering up the day. In the
kitchen I put on my shoes, new ones, wide enough for my square
feet and nothing at all like the shoes I wore for the last forty years
of my working life. I feel their heft, their anchoring embrace of
my feet and I love tying my laces. I learned to tie my laces beside
my mother's big hospital bed in the sunroom of our house, and I
remember my feeling of triumph when I accomplished it under
her gaze. Most of my memories of my mother are like photographs and I don't entirely trust them. But this one is truly inside
of me, like a little folded note.

I say to Peter, "I love my life."

He looks up from his newspaper as if a little of that golden
pear glow has rubbed off on him for a moment. "That's a wonderful thing to be able to say."

It is true; I wonder if lots of people feel this way most of the
time. A veil of sadness that I have been thrashing away at for a
lifetime, like a spider's web that is always back in the morning,
has been lifted. Or maybe that piece of my soul has found its way
home.

I hear from Ruthie that Linc is now in Bridgewater State Hospital, the prison for criminals who are too mentally ill to be with

the general prison population, even in the iso unit. His father is his legal guardian and the only person allowed to visit him. He reports that Linc is happier here than in the Middlesex Jail. He's on completely different meds, Lithium and Prozac and his parents are puzzled by the seeming randomness of the way he's been medicated. His mother says that the two assault cases against him in Massachusetts are pending and the DA wants to give him ten years for one. Her theory is that he is afraid of being sent to North Carolina to serve his sentence and so is sabotaging that possibility by his behavior. I wonder if he received my last letter or if it's wandering around the prison system.

Mark tells me that when Linc was first incarcerated in Bridgewater they did not allow prisoners to have any books beyond a bible. They just sat in isolation with nothing to do all day. Mark and Ruthie couldn't believe it and kept pressing to have Linc be allowed books.

"Well, I suppose we could have a little library," the warden finally said. So they started one.

In the 1930s Bridgewater was a farm for short-term prisoners, where they could work outside all day. Summer travelers driving along Route 28 from the Cape were captured by the romantic view of prison life as hinted at by the rolling fields and visible farm life. Then in 1970 Frederick Wiseman made Bridgewater famous with the film *Titicut Follies*, following prisoners around for twenty-nine days, revealing them naked in their cells, and force fed by their keepers. Men were simply forgotten there. I trust that it is more humane now, but the library story is telling. The Bridgewater website looks strangely homemade, with a long list of things you cannot wear if you are visiting inmates: tank tops, short skirts, wrap around skirts, army fatigues, black pants and white shirts (for men). It seems to be written by someone named Heather, who doesn't do very well at putting together an English sentence. Not long ago they cut down every last tree on the hospital property because a prisoner escaped the building and climbed into one. Mark says they have put up macabre giant plastic vultures to keep the geese away. The place has been made hideous. Last month the death of an inmate who was being subdued by guards was ruled a homicide.

Finally I am allowed to see Linc. He is out of the intensive treatment unit. I make the ninety-minute drive south on a Wednesday afternoon. The complex is off Route 24, invisible from the road now, with an eerie new growth pine forest around it. There are many buildings at Bridgewater: jails, treatment centers and combinations of the two. Linc is in the state prison hospital at the end of the road, a long low collection of buildings wrapped in a tangled mass of barbed wire with a small opening at the entrance.

I go in and am directed to fill out a form, park my belongings in a locker, and wait. Another woman is waiting with me and shares her tales of previous visits, long waits with access to her son sometimes denied. It is freezing cold in the waiting room. After forty minutes a guard opens the door and I am passed through the metal detector and escorted into the complex. We pass through a series of slamming steel gates until we are out in the center of the hexagonal complex, in a field, crossing to another entrance. Then more slamming steel gates, and a corridor with a few hospital inmates in dark blue cinder block cells. It must have been a paint sale; you could go mad just looking at this color.

At the end of the corridor Linc is waiting in a cage set in the corner of a room with computers and a table. My escort sits down on a stool outside the door and I go up to Linc and hold his hands through the bars. He has grown a beard, dark reddish brown, very handsome. He looks like I imagine Christ.

We begin our visit.

"We call this the birdcage," says Linc cheerfully. He is clearly happy to see me, to have the monotony broken. He seems better than I have ever seen him before. Less nervous, less intense. They are giving his medication by injection so he can't cheat. I am thinking how strange it is that I have grown accustomed to these visits, that I am oddly matter-of-fact about it all now. We banter together. He tells me minute by minute what he does with his day. Lots of sleeping, a shower, meals that get passed through a slot into his cell. Two hundred and fifty pushups a day. Reading. A ball of stuffing for Thanksgiving. No radio allowed.

He is scheduled to be taken down to North Carolina within a week, so this will be the last time I will see him for a long while. I ask him how he's feeling about going.

"Well, I'm excited for the change. Maybe I'll get to go out-doors some for yard work or learn some new skills. And this is the beginning of serving the manslaughter sentence, so I should get out in six years. Then I'll go to a halfway house for a while and get a job, maybe selling newspapers. I wrote a nine page letter to George in the Boat Yard, telling him I'd work for five dollars a day for ten years when I get out."

"But I'm nervous about who the guys are going to be in North Carolina. Just have to remember to mind my own business and pick my friends carefully. It's a mostly black population; I'm a little nervous about that."

Digging for things to talk about, I tell him about the service at my black church the Sunday before, and about Reverend Atu White's sermon on Job.

"He has the most amazing style of preaching. He looked out at us, and said 'Job is hard for me, I struggled with this one, and I'm still struggling, so bear with me.' And then he paces back and forth and doesn't say anything for a long time, like he's waiting for God to speak to him. And then he says something and lots of aahs come from the crowd, and he says something else after a minute. It's like we're right there with him, figuring out why God gave Job to Satan and let him take away everything he had. You should read Job, Linc. He reminds me of you."

"I will. I'll read it tonight." I know he was serious in that in-tention. I wonder what he will make of Job.

"Sometimes," I continue, "when you don't know what to do, just don't do anything. Just be still for a bit and ask God. It's amazing how the answer just flies back when you can just clear the mental space." I can't believe I'm saying this to him. I suppose it can't hurt. He is at my mercy when it comes to listening.

"Do they have any kind of services here?" I ask him.

"A woman comes once a week, and if you go three times she gives you a rosary. I think it's all Catholic. But I can't go anyway. They keep me away from everyone."

He had talked to Noah the night before and was full of fatherly pride in his son, hope for his future. They seem oddly about the same age to me, he and Noah.

After an hour my head is aching from the visual confusion of looking at his face through steel bars, or maybe from the intensity of the conversation. I hold his hands and say a prayer with him before I leave. The guard says to me, "you know the way out, right?"

"I guess…"

"Just go to the end of the corridor, through the doors, and then through the next doors, out across the plaza and into the next building."

"OK…" And I set out. Through the first set of doors I panic. I am locked in, between these two great mechanized steel doors and my heart begins to pound. I can't breathe. The guard looks through the window and mouths "hold on" and he opens the door and escorts me out through the maze. I am suddenly very eager to get as far away as possible. As I go back through the waiting room, I see my friend is still waiting to see her son, an hour and a half later.

An email comes to me one day, long after I have finished combing the archives in Northampton for any whiff of Erastus's life. It is from Steve Strimer, the local expert on the Underground Railroad who was convinced, early on, that Erastus was an agent of the UGRR in Northampton. He writes "I have had a hunch for awhile that Erastus's house was still up on King Street. I think I've found it. I plan to check the deeds on Monday but I'm attaching the map evidence as a pdf.

"The house has undergone fairly disastrous renovations over the years but retains all its lines and the front door is pretty amazing. I'll send you pictures soon." The next email says: "The WHOLE HOUSE is still there. It's the Rectory of the Catholic Church. And they are planning to demolish it. There is a stop order that expires in two months."

I am stunned. How could I have missed the house. I had stood right in front of it and said to myself, "this must be where the house once was." But it was nothing like a house built in 1824, and it didn't occur to me that the Catholic Church had simply lopped off the verandas and clad the house in brick, making it look like something built in 1984. A rowdy committee of determined historians has formed in Northampton to save the house from the Diocese's plan to build a community hall on the site. One says he will personally lie down in front of the wrecking ball. I will happily join him. There is something devilishly mischievous in Erastus's house being the rectory of the St. Elizabeth Ann Seton Parish of the Catholic Church.

XXI

Mr. Nobody

MY GRANDSON EAMON SAYS, "OMA, CAN BOOKS DIE?" He is three and a half and all his friends are shooting things. He seems to be thinking about what all that means.

"No," I say, "only living things can die." And we begin a recitation of living things: mama, and papa and his dog, and ants and bees and birds. And plants.

"When we get home let's plant a seed in some dirt," I say to him. "It's alive, but it's sleeping, and if you put it in dirt with some water it wakes up and becomes a plant after a while." In the kitchen I spill a package of basil seeds into his chubby little hand. "You be the holder, and I'll pick them out one by one and put them in these little pots of dirt. Then you can water them for me." He squats beside me and his curly blond head bends over the seeds which he examines with great concentration. I can see his mind working over these ideas of life and death.

My mind has been working on them too. My friend Jean in Louisiana has just died of liver cancer, the friend whose husband's freshly dug grave I had visited just a few months ago. She and August Wilson died of the same disease. She held it at bay for a long time, but then I think she just lost her reason to live. She is the first of my close friends to have died and I am shocked that death can happen so quickly, that there was no time to tell her I loved her. She would have hated that anyway. One day she went to the hospital and the next she was in a coma. Three weeks later she was dead. Her mother called me when it was all over. She is ninety-five.

My conversation with Eamon on the subject of life and death has just begun. It's not as black and white as one might think. I notice that Eamon has a funny way of sometimes calling people "Mr. Nobody" and I have just figured out that he is trying out ways to deal with the fact that people come and go. He's calling them "Mr. I'm not sure you're really here." Peter goes away a lot and gets this "Mr. Nobody" title more than most of us. I am thinking that the reason he goes away a lot is so that he gets to be the leaver rather than the left. His parents travelled a lot, left him a lot, so now he gets to be in control. In my case, the leaving was just once but forever, when my mother died. "Get over it," Peter periodically says to me, "it happened fifty years ago." Maybe I almost have.

Peter went to Atlanta on Sunday, came home on Monday and went to San Francisco for a week on Tuesday. On Peter's one night home I picked a fight with him, just so I could be mad instead of sad. The fight was over his determined, ongoing refusal to have a cell phone. So he is truly gone when he leaves. Truly in control. We have played this roulette of attachment and abandonment for thirty years. Loving someone turns out to be the bravest thing we ever do in life.

We are approaching the end of the decade, the decade that began with Peter's departure to Kansas City and my first encounters with Erastus's letters. The country is in a very somber mood. Our breakfast table has become the scene of a daily dirge as Peter reads *The Boston Globe* and *The New York Times*. The news itself is terrible. The poor are getting poorer, the rich have shamelessly legalized their piracy, and the country seems to have stepped into a bog, lost its way. I listen to my husband's gloomy commentary and I keep feeling my feet on the floor. Why am I not sharing his despair? My optimism provokes him to paraphrase Voltaire: "Optimists are just pessimists who have more to learn."

In our retirement our differences are more pronounced. Peter is a restless wanderer; I am a burrower, finding the Holy Spirit in the garden and the grandchildren. Sometimes I go to church, sometimes I don't. Eamon has rebelled against church since the day I took him to Sunday school and he had to say his name out loud in front of all the children. When he was very little he just absorbed the spirit and rocked with the music, but he has begun to notice that he is a separate being, powerless to invoke invisibility. Are our children born of the Holy Ghost? Unwillingly made into flesh? Erastus has put it in my head that I need to keep that spiritual spark alive and conscious in the next generation; that the world is full of devilish things. It's like a sacred vessel that needs to be carried with care, and yet I'm not quite sure what the shape of the vessel is that I'm trying to hand on. Or exactly what's in it. Maybe it is the mossy forest on Dog Island Point and the barking seals on Fight Ledge.

Among Erastus's papers in the Northampton archives is a transcribed copy of the diary of Esther Edwards, Erastus's grandmother and Jonathan Edward's oldest sister.

This must have been one of the vessels that came to him, a family treasure that he must have read with care. There is a notation that the original diary was kept from 1717 to 1726 on little scraps of paper, grocery receipts and the like, that were tied up in a bundle. The transcription was made sometime after Erastus's death, typed with care by an unknown ancestor in the late nineteenth or early twentieth century. It comes to eighty-five pages and is a daily contemplation of how present or absent the Lord has been in her life that day. On page two she writes: "I had some quickenings & earnest desires after Christ..., but the next day was very dull & dead. My Father preached ... My heart Stil continued very much unaffected & senceless..." But later she writes "I am now returned from Boston...when I was upon my journey down, God remarkably met with me twice...: riding after ye Sun was up and Seeing ye dew hang butifully on ye Pine bows it Brought to mind y't (that) precious promise I will be as ye dew unto Israel with a very refreshing and Sweet relish…I almost forgot where I was and what I was about."

I am comforted to know that God came to Esther in the early morning light, but she was insensible to him in church. She was on constant spiritual alert and found the spirit in unexpected places, just like Erastus and I. But to create the space for the spirit to enter, you must empty yourself of all the stuff and buzzing. Maybe the essence of the vessel is emptiness.

This must be the essence of faith: the sure knowledge that you are filled with the universe, ticking along as steadily as the bees and the hummingbirds, until it's time to take up God's next assignment. I am on the front line now: there is no one left in my parents' generation. There is power in this seniority, and maybe I'll have it to use for another quarter century.

Hannah has found an apartment and is moving out. She has worked hard for this moment and I love the little place she has found, full of sunlight and quiet. She and Linc will both be moving on in their lives in the same week. A new season.

XXII

My heart aches there are
so many little folks in it…

I AM GOING ON A TWO-WEEK HOLIDAY TO VIEQUES, an island in the Caribbean, with Linc's parents, Mark and Ruthie, and longtime mutual friends, Nancy and John. Peter is going off to San Francisco. He gets too bored on desert islands.

On the jetway I hear Ruthie's throaty low voice behind me and I turn around. Who's that with her, that guy with a big guitar case and a mass of reddish curls? Could only be Noah. Ruthie flashes her great smile and says, not quite sotto voce enough: "We got the word yesterday. His school put him on a leave of absence. He's a little depressed." I smile and greet him, warmly I hope, all the while thinking: where's he going to sleep? With me? Just what we need: a morose fifteen year old skulking around.

We take our separate seats and seven hours later are climbing out of a six-seater on the hot Vieques tarmac. Mark is ahead of us, organizing the cars and soon we have a caravan bouncing up the rugged hills toward Pilon where we have rented "Touchstone."

Nancy, beside me in the back seat, says, "What are we going to do with Noah? We can't have him in the living room. He'll want to sleep in the morning."

"Let's just wait til we see how the place is configured," I say.

The solution is to take a mattress from the second bed in my room and put it on the floor of Mark and Ruthie's room. We give them the biggest and best room to make up for it. Noah has decided to wander off and play his guitar out on the rocks looking over the Caribbean surf. Ruthie is watching him out of the corner of her eye. The doctor said not to let him out of her sight, she tells Nancy and me.

But Noah seems like a normal teenager to me. He wanders in and out of the house like a minstrel singing "House of the Rising Sun" and "Stewball." He's tall and weighs 153 pounds which I happen to know because Cape Air demands that information quite publicly of all its passengers. He has that white concave chest of a slouching man/boy going straight down into a pair of blue jean shorts that would surely drop to the floor without a belt. He has a soft reddish fuzz on his face. He's cute. His smile is a mile wide and he's great at conversing with adults. No sulky teenager here.

At dinner the first night Nancy recounts an amazing story of how she became Brian Epstein's (manager of the Beatles) secretary in the sixties by lying about her shorthand abilities. She had the job when the world went wild over the Beatles and when Brian Epstein went off to his country house and committed suicide. Noah sits with his jaw wide open whispering "are you serious?"

We are six around a glass dinner table, looking out on the scrubby Vieques hills and the turquoise expanse of the Caribbean beyond. After dinner Noah gets his guitar and a crumbled piece of paper on which he has written a song. Nancy is telling a story now of going out to California and trying to launch her singing career. "It was really hard, and in the end I just wasn't tough enough." Moving toward the dishes, she breaks into a couple of bars of "Gonna get along without you now," snapping her fingers and knocking me right back into my teens.

Then Noah smooths out his piece of paper and begins to play the mournful song he has written. We are all suddenly, very carefully, listening. And when he finishes we clap, enthusiastically, but he has picked up on our vibe. The song is a little limp, his voice tight, with a strained quality to it that he will probably outgrow.

Nancy talks a little more about how tough it is to break into the music world. I mutter something about how hard it has been to learn to paint. And Noah is gone. To his room. Mark and Ruthie follow him. Nancy and I do the dishes.

By the third night Noah is working on getting Mark to let him have a glass of wine. John is for it. Mark against, but he finally relents. It goes on like that. Noah is always testing what he can get away with, deeply attracted to our sybaritic, beachcomber adult life, which we had not expected to have scrutinized by a "depressed" teenager.

I am a little worried about this "depression" but in truth this doesn't look like any depression I've ever seen. This kid is having fun. He likes these adults. He's listening to every word we say. He's asking me to define turgid, concupiscent. We play in the surf for hours, talking non-stop. He wants to know everything about my life, and especially about all the mistakes I've made.

He loves his Grandmother. Adores her. Wraps his arms around her. Protects her, carries her luggage. Responds to her signals. To me it seems like she is the depressed one. Her voice doesn't have its former range, as though she cannot quite get enough breath. But watching them together I realize that Noah is the great gift, the late redemption of her life.

One night Noah has an opportunity to jam with some guys in a bar. Open mike—though carefully controlled by the owner. Noah has an acoustic guitar, a Gibson. He needs an electric guitar for this crowd and I watch him flash his charming grin and finger a few chords. Before long a middle-aged hippie has adopted Noah and relinquished his red electric Les Paul for him to play. Mark buys the guy a drink, probably to guarantee that Noah will in fact get to play the guitar. We listen to a series of middle-aged men stand at the mike, some so wasted they just sway a little. One does a few notes of Johnny Cash. A harmonica player is good, but it is a sad parade. They were all fifteen once. They all had big dreams. Finally the leader signals to Noah, who has a few words with the guys, cluing them into the key, I suppose. And then he starts. The sound tears through the room. The conversation at the back, behind the mid-room bar, stops. People begin to cheer. Noah thunders on, his hands racing up and down the neck of the red guitar. The woman beside me gives a thumbs-up. On the other side of her someone holds up a cell phone and yells into it "You gotta hear this. It's just a kid. He's unbelievable."

After eight minutes or so he lets the harmonica player in and begins to wind down, smiling a little, trying to be nonchalant.

I know that night is going to be a turning point for him. Maybe the whole week. Two nights later I am walking along the Malecon, the boardwalk of Esperanza, with him. Four different groups stop us. "Hey, you're that kid that played at Moe's Azul the other night. You're fantastic kid. I know we're going to hear more about you." Yes, we're going to hear more about Noah.

★ ★ ★

In my living room are gathered the trustees of our home in Maine: my siblings, step and half, and my three Emerson first cousins, including Linc's mother Ruthie. My older brother, Jon, who fled from Betty to the West Coast when he was seventeen, still lives there fifty years later, and I am his proxy. We are assembled to work out the next step of passing responsibility in the management of the property to our children. The gray midday surrounds the house like a posse that has herded us here and the house holds us in its delicate layering of familial time: grandma's bright cherry highboy looking down on Eamon's yellow rocking horse. On the mahogany mantelpiece Erastus is commanding the room, looking down on us, his arms akimbo.

I introduce him. "This is the guy. The one I've been writing about." I am feeling shy about this. I have become well known in the family for my odd obsession with this ancestor. I tell them about Norman Boas and the papers and the ripped portrait, languishing in his basement for years. We are all quiet for a bit, looking at him and then at each other. And then everyone starts talking at once, pointing out who has the rectangular forehead and who has the slanting eyebrows. We are all there in his face, and so are our children. Even Linc has his eyes. The civility of four generations sharing a summer home comes from him, and so, somehow, does the family chapel.

On Thanksgiving morning Peter and I hang the portrait in the dining room. I was all ready to hang it over my bed, but one day Peter murmured that he was "willing to consider" granting Erastus a place in the dining room next to my grandmother, Josephine Sewall. I climb up on a ladder in a great warm dust-filled shaft of sunlight and hook the curvy brass S into the molding and let Erastus float next to the window.

"Too high," says Peter. I move him six inches lower and climb down the ladder. We step back. The room is alive with light playing on these two faces of ancestors who never knew each other but are nonetheless woven together through their descendants. They look out at us as though with fresh expectations, not from the terminus of lives with grief and disappointments, of diminishing health and eyes on the almighty. They are looking out intently at us, waiting for the party to begin.

I found a long letter in the Northampton archives from Grandma Josephine to Aunt Sadie, that skinny little granddaughter with the straight blond hair in the window of Erastus's heart. Like her Aunt Sallie, Nettie's older sister, Sadie lived a long life as a single woman, a very beautiful single woman. I suspect that she may have had one of those "Boston marriages." I know that two of my cousins will be gleeful at this speculation, having both "come out" recently. First Andy and then, two years later, his mother. Sallie and Sadie left lots of letters for the clever and motivated reader to embellish with their own imagined detail. Their long-gone shoulders are still silently waiting for us to lean on if we go seeking them. But theirs does not seem to be my story. I will leave that reflecting pond for others to look in.

This Thanksgiving morning has that still, pregnant feeling of all Thanksgiving mornings. Expectant. Redolent of temptations to come. The shopping has been done; the kitchen is saturated with the smell of apple pies baked the night before. A few odd outliers of the family are in their rooms upstairs, come to us as the keepers of the big old family. My son-in-law has been brining the Turkey for twenty-four hours and brings it over to stuff and put in the oven early in the morning. We have an affable cup of coffee together.

For Andrew I am the ancestor, so to speak, on his wife's side of the family. He never knew Betty or my father. He was not here four years ago for the first Thanksgiving without Betty, who was too afflicted with dementia to be with us. All the children in their twenties and thirties danced around the table in unrestrained glee. No more martinis on demand, the straying hand that sidles up to her neighbor's glass of wine.

Even though she is now long dead, Betty can still give me a sharp kick in the solar plexus.

"I don't want that bad energy in my food," says Hannah when she feels my old housewifely anxiety rising.

They all begin to gather, Eamon and Margaret are running in circles around the kitchen, weaving their way through the potato mashers. I note that Eamon has a jersey with a big grinning elk on the front. A shaman friend of mine has determined that an elk is my power animal and warned me that I would now see them everywhere. Peter is mixing the Bloody Marys and greeting cousins coming in the door. Hannah, without the boyfriend of last year, is hanging back in her upstairs room. She imagines gossip. "Gossip, Mama, is what people say about you that they wouldn't want you to know they said." That covers a lot of conversation. Peter's brother and his wife come down from their room and chase the grandchildren until Eamon begins to cry. It is all the normal hubbub that makes this house feel like a sanctuary, like an album collecting its stories.

We carve the turkey and pile the plates high. It is mid afternoon and the brightness of morning has turned murky, ready to receive candlelight and rainbows streaming from the chandelier. The table is filled to capacity: twelve of us reach out and take each other's hands. Erastus in his new position looks me directly in the eye as I sit at the end of the Thanksgiving table. The twelve of us sing the Doxology and say grace, with the children at a little table in the corner of the room watching us curiously.

Looking up at Erastus's portrait, Jody says, "He is a little Dumbledoreish," referring to Harry Potter's wise wizard of a headmaster. I know what she means. Harry's portraits come quite alive. Erastus feels that way to me too—like he might tap me on the shoulder and ask for a plate of turkey at any moment. In April he'll be 200 years old, just in time for Easter.

Linc was picked up at the crack of dawn one winter morning in January 2011 by two sheriffs from North Carolina who had flown up to collect him at Bridgewater. I can see the three of them in the cold fluorescent prison light, stuttering through a series of slamming steel doors, out through the gritty black snow hedges and ruffles of barbed wire. He was up long before they came, waiting. He'd put on the special clothes they'd given him for travel. Like a boy on his first trip to camp, his dread must have been overpowered by the succulence of something new. A whole day in company. The sun. The moving landscape. His first glimpse of a GPS system. He has been in isolation in Massachusetts prisons for seven years.

And the two men? Were they fearful of this notorious fellow? Were they wearing all the trappings of their authority? The pistols and badges and tall black boots? Maybe not. Linc wrote that it was an "inconspicuous operation." He wore a legbrace on his left leg "to keep me from running" and handcuffs concealed under a big red windbreaker.

They had breakfast at Dunkin Donuts. The Tour d'Argent of travelling prisoners. I can feel the joy rising from the page as he writes. He savors every detail down to the bus trip to the parking lot where Lt. Novack's car was parked. They left the "other gentleman" at his home.

"I am here (in Central Prison) in Mental Health West Room 414. My room has all white walls with shelves and a table stretching out of the wall. There is a long window above my bed only about seven inches wide and it's fogged up so I can't see out only if its day or night." He just landed a janitor's job and he's made some friends. His day has structure and people in it. He gets up early to do his work. There's TV and a "Rec Room" with puzzles and games in which he may spend an hour a day. Every Friday they get to watch a movie and have popcorn and coffee. He recites to me all the things he can buy at the canteen. Batteries for only 19 cents! Candy bars! Is it possible that the treatment of mentally ill prisoners could be so different in two states of the Union?

Nonetheless he is lonely, far away from his family and suddenly cut off from phone contact. There is just one call a year allowed from this prison, at Christmas. His lifeline to his New England family has been cut and he is sinking in a sea of southern accents he can hardly understand. His whole family is stunned and suddenly confronted with relearning an old skill: letter writing. Two days after I get Linc's first letter I get a second, enclosing some permission-to-visit forms, just in case I should ever get to North Carolina.

Still, he seems to have made some friends: two long termers in for murder. One is a sixty-five year old man named Ed McKenna who has been in the North Carolina system for thirty-two years for killing a policeman in a housebreak. He thinks Linc will be sent to a minimum security prison to serve his sentence. He's an artist, knowledgable about copyright law. He designed the airplane on the "First in Flight" North Carolina license plate.

I feel a little leaping of my heart as I read this. Linc is describing a possible mentor. I don't care if he is doing life for murder. He's got stuff to teach. And Linc is a sponge ready to soak it up. A lot of stuff gets picked up in prison, most of it not what a mother would want. But still this is a system where something, a skill or a bit of knowledge, might be learned. And Linc is resilient. His letters are a testament to that, and to his ability to make structure out of emptiness, to find pleasure in work, and joy in a little popcorn and company, even in a third great grandfather who died a century and a half ago.

XXIII

I Could Write an Uncle Tom's Cabin

IT'S BEEN TWO YEARS SINCE I'VE BEEN TO NORTHAMPTON. In a dreary spring rain I head back to the Connecticut River Valley west of Boston. The last time I made this trip I was a solitary researcher, trying to piece together a long forgotten life. This time I am going to meet with the "Hopkins team," a group that has formed spontaneously to preserve what has turned out to be one of the few surviving Underground Railroad "safehouses" in the Northampton area. Erastus has been my private spiritual mentor for almost a decade and now he has suddenly become the lost hero of an entire community. He is important to each member of this team of preservationists, historians and educators for their own reasons, quite different from mine. I think I'm happy about this, but I'm not sure. It means I have to share him, and that what I treasure about him most, his complex humanity as a parent, may be overshadowed by his hitherto secret role in the Underground Railroad.

Each member of this unusual group is going through a telescoped experience of what I have been through over the last ten years: putting Erastus's life together, one piece at a time. They are having the same thrill of the hunt, and of discovery. All of us have come together to see if we can save his house from demolition, and to evaluate whether it might have a future as an interpretive site for the Underground Railroad.

Leading the team is Steve Strimer whom I first talked to five years ago over the din of the copy machine in his printing cooperative in Florence, a village of Northampton. He told me then that he suspected that Erastus was one of the leaders of the Underground Railroad in Northampton. But it was not until several months ago, when the letter from Erastus to his nephew about the slave "Bill" surfaced, that there was clear proof. Steve has been tracking down the fugitive slave story of Northampton and Florence, Massachusetts for the last eighteen years, and he is passionate about the subject, but he is also a clearheaded negotiator who wants to keep everyone moving toward the same goals—including the Catholic Church which owns the house.

Working closely with him is Bruce Laurie, an emeritus professor of history at the University of Massachusetts at Amherst. In his *Beyond Garrison: Anti-Slavery and Social Reform* he works to restore the balance of fame between William Lloyd Garrison and the many quiet and not-so-quiet leaders of the abolitionist movement who were Garrison's contemporaries. Bruce first encountered Erastus in the *Reminiscences of Old Northampton*, by Henry S. Gere, the editor and owner of the Hampshire Gazette for fifty-seven years. By Bruce's assessment Gere and Erastus worked together in tandem for many years for the abolition of slavery and ultimately for the development of the Republican party as a single-issue, anti-slavery party. Bruce's book *Rebels in Paradise* (published in January of 2015) includes a chapter on Erastus.

Finally, I am able to see, through the eyes of a political historian who has carefully pieced together the complex evidence, Erastus's development from his youthful employment by the American Colonization Society to his radical abolitionist stance. Bruce compares Erastus to Lincoln, saying that like Lincoln his positions on slavery evolved "but faster and farther." Like Lincoln he abandoned Colonization, but long before him. "He was an inspiring speaker, a serious student of history and politics who, like Lincoln, appealed to the 'better angels' in people with stirring intellectual excursions into the nation's idealistic tradition." But

Erastus's health failed when he was still quite young. In September of 1855, Bruce finds him "sidelined" with another bout of hypertension. He was only forty-five.

Bruce found Erastus's article "An Appeal to the Voters of Hampshire County" in Gere's *Gazette*. It highlights his position on "nativism," the anti-immigrant stance that plagued 19th century American politics. In summary he asks, "why punish foreigners? Why deny them their "acknowledged rights to humanity?" How can a party ask for their support if it discriminates against them and denies the basic doctrine "that all men are born free and equal?"

I am stunned as I read this to see that two of us, at opposite ends of the State, have been looking at some of the same microfiche. Bruce has, for years, been carefully assembling a huge political puzzle, and he knows the meaning of these little slivers of Erastus and just where to put them. He has the public man and I, the private.

The Northampton Historical Commission, (the "conscience of Northampton," when it comes to fighting the obliteration of history in favor of profits and progress) is excited about the recent discoveries and some of their members are clearly on "the team," as are members of The David Ruggles Center, recently established to study the Underground Railroad in Florence and African-American history in the area. One of these, Lisa Baskin, has offered to put me up for the night.

She has given me directions. As I travel through the foggy meadows, I watch for the landmark she has described, a big white barn. It looms up suddenly in front of me, the biggest barn I have ever seen. Approaching the house, I feel like I have come back a century to a more lovable America. The doorway is framed by a large lilac, blooming in the mist. Bronze sculptures have been placed, with clear and tender attention, in several spots at the entry. A solidly resting human form lies near the front walk, as though inviting you to rest here too. I wonder who this Lisa Baskin is. Does she rent part of this great house?

I ring the bell and the door opens. Two Jack Russell terriers greet me with wild enthusiasm, framed by a woman of about my age with dark curls and olive skin.

"Off, Cal," she commands and Cal stops in mid air. "Cal's just a puppy and I'm trying to train him not to leap up like that. This is Rosa, his mother. You're ok with dogs?"

"Oh yes." I kneel and give Cal what you might call a leg-pit scratch which I know from experience makes a dog an instant friend.

"Everyone on the team is so excited that you've come to Northampton," Lisa says, and I am startled at this idea. "And I am especially pleased that you're staying with me. Come in and I'll take you up to your room so you can settle your things in. We have to be at City Hall for the meeting of the Historical Commission at 5:30, so we just have time for tea."

As we go up the narrow old staircase I am guessing that this house was built, at least in part, in the 18th century, and I am also remembering a print in my office, long ago, of an artist named Leonard Baskin.

"Are you an artist?" I ask.

"No, my husband was," Lisa replies.

"Leonard Baskin? I ask a little timidly.

"Yes."

The work is stunning. The house is amazing. My mind is in overdrive trying to take in all of the artwork, the books, the extraordinary material objects carefully placed on every available surface. She has led me to a sweet guestroom with a canopied four-poster bed, furnished in early Erastus. I feel the quickening heart that comes with the invisible soft touch of history.

We go downstairs to the library to have tea. Not just the mug of tea I would plunk in front of my guests, but an entire silver platter of tea paraphenalia, from Meissen china cups and pot to clotted cream, scones and gobs of velvety red jam.

I would like to have more to report here, but in truth I was made speechless by the library. We are in a room about thirty by forty feet, with twenty-foot ceilings and bookcases on all four walls, filled with leather antique books on one side of the room and art books opposite, all stacked two deep. There is one high window but otherwise the room is lit by nine incandescent lamps with ivory shades casting a very library-like warm light. Every surface is covered with bronze sculptures or New England ephemera, like bronze medals and death cameos. The effect, overall, is breathtaking. Lisa eases me out of my speechlessness with the information that she is a collector.

"All the books on this side have something to do with women. The earliest is from Europe in the fifteenth century, a book typeset by a woman. Some of them are written by women, but many were created in some other way by a woman, either typeset or illustrated or designed. I have a special interest in African-American, working women, and social justice issues relating to women."

We drink our tea and talk, and I tell her the story of my coming upon Erastus's letters. She is a woman who makes easy connections and we hit it off right away. On the tea table before me is a beautiful small bronze human figure, arching back on one arm, reminding me that I need to do this occasionally.

At the Northampton City Hall we sit in what feels like a hearing room. The group is tiny; the news of the finding of Erastus's house has not yet leaked out to a broader public. Each member of the "Hopkins team" comes to the podium. As the out-of-town guest I go first and tell the story you have just read, of a man who loved his family, who wrote them beautiful letters. I tell them about the scarlet fever epidemic in 1854 that took the lives of Lottie and Johnnie, of Caro's death from dysentery—and little Willie's fatal scalding accident in bath water too hot. (Bruce Laurie stopped in his tracks when I told him about Willie. "Garrison lost his son in exactly the same way.")

Moving on in Erastus's career, I tell them about the Northampton State Hospital and Linc. (History keeps coming around and trying to tell us something.) The Northampton State Hospital was a dramatic presence in this community for more than a century. Now most of it has been obliterated, but the continuing dilemma of the seriously mentally ill is ever-present. For many years this hospital was a model institution, until it was overwhelmed by numbers of patients beyond its capacity. Someone on the committee tells me that some pieces of the State Hospital have been preserved, but the town hasn't yet figured out how to make sense of them to the public. This is another thread to be "interpreted" should the house find new life.

I have rarely had an audience so spellbound. They are fascinated by this man who has just walked out of history and into their lives, just as surely as if he were ambling down Main Street. They have been primed by reading the letter that Erastus wrote on July 11, 1859 to his nephew in Vermont, the letter that accompanied the fugitive slave "Bill" on his clandestine trip from Erastus's house at 112 King Street to Chatham, Ontario. Like the letter that Paul wrote to Philemon, passing on the slave Onesimus, this one was treasured and saved because it was "freighted with meaning."

The house is apparently one of the few remaining houses in Northampton known to have been a harbor for fugitive slaves. Tom Weiner, a sixth-grade teacher in a school across the street, speaks after me, about the power of this house to bring alive to his students the real meaning of the Underground Railroad. "There is nothing in the world that could do this in the same way as the real thing," he says, "it would be a stunning addition to the resources of this city for our children. And I can tell you, every school teacher in the whole area will be here beside me saying the same thing when news of this gets out."

When our part of the meeting is over Lisa and I decamp to a local Chinese restaurant, the Great Wall, and over the course of the next half hour the rest of the team joins us until we are like an overflowing Chinese family all talking at once. I am trying to listen to six conversations, each of them hinting at another bit of Erastus's life. Bruce says that Erastus was provoked to speak against the Holy Cross Charter by their excessive demands.

Steve has concluded that Erastus used his presidency of the Connecticut River Railroad to get fugitive slaves to Canada, probably having aid from workers on the trains. One bit of evidence for this is that Seth Hunt, who was Treasurer of the Railroad and eventually succeeded Erastus as President, was a known agent. Then there are the practical discussions of whether the house might be moved and what organizations could unite to make use of it as an interpretive and administrative space.

Later in the evening, Lisa and I continue our conversation in the beautiful library. After a bit she says to me, "Since you are a writer, you might be interested in this," and she leads me over to the corner of the room, to a blue-grey wooden desk with a painting of a woman blowing a horn, the goddess Juno, on the top.

"It was Virginia Woolf's. She used it until 1929 when she gave it to her nephew. He did the painting." Lisa is brilliantly sparse and matter-of-fact describing the provenance of this remarkable object.

If this were in a museum I would dare not touch it, but here in this reverent library I reach out and brush my hand across the surface. It is a profoundly intimate object and I can feel the struggles that have gone on in its presence, the moments of delicious achievement, and sometimes despair.

Sitting with Lisa in the library, I feel that same sense of comfort that surrounded me at Norman Boas's house, the comfort of knowing the past is all around you, carefully catalogued, remembered and loved. Lisa's passion for all that surrounds us shows through in her very understated manner, as if she is constantly holding herself in check. It's like a fast pulse in the room. She shows me a little more of her collection, including a delicate handwritten letter from Harriet Beecher Stowe for Sojourner Truth, promoting her *Narrative*.

When I wake in the morning, I lie in the four-poster bed wiggling my toes in a slot in the middle of the footboard. A bundling board must once have slipped into it, dividing this cozy space into two. I feel the warm intensity of the history in this house, like the exhalation of a sweet breath.

The next day six of us go for our "walk through" of the house at 112 King Street. We are guided by Eileen Sullivan, the church secretary. Father O'Connor, the parish priest, greets us briefly.

"Please, if you find any memento of your family you would like," he says to me, "we would love you to have it." I feel for him, he just wants a parish hall for his church, and this is all an unexpected pain in the neck. How did a whole city overlook this "treasure" for a century and a half?

The house has been unoccupied for the past year, though some of the church furnishings are still in place. We go in through the kitchen, which is very 1950s, with simple honey-colored wooden cabinets, including a whole floor-to-ceiling wall of them that must have stored supplies for church suppers. But the ceiling itself has the original stamped tin and in a flash I can see the children bouncing through here on their way out to the long gone barn. In a little handwritten diary I found in the attic in Maine, Nettie describes in a breathless, unpunctuated paragraph, the busy day of an eight-year old living in this house in 1856. On Thursday: "When I got dressed I went down to breakfast, after that I rode on the pony, and then went to school. I walked on the gas pipes after school, I played horse with Lemm and Carol and then went to dinner, after that we played old hundred and then went to school, after that we went to ride and then played paper dolls then went to supper then read then went to bed." Running in and out, right through this kitchen door, red hair flying, screen door slamming.

Railroad tracks run behind the house, the tracks of Erastus's railroad, as Steve reminds me. The right-of-way has now been turned into a bicycle trail, though passenger trains are coming back to Northampton soon. The house has been lived in by single priests for more than a century, but it is not hard to imagine Erastus's family here. As our group walks through we are examining the architectural details to figure out what changes have been made. Across from the kitchen, the dining room where Nettie raced home to take her midday dinner, has been redone in a 1920s dark walnut style suitable for priestly dining, but it would have been the same size and shape, probably decorated in a gay paper of the time.

The room to the left of the front door must have been Erastus's library and across the hall, the parlor where Willie's little coffin once rested. The leaded glass in the side panels of the front door is original and the curving staircase that leads us to the second floor has new ugly balusters, but also a lovely niche near the top. I wonder what was in it in Erastus's time.

There would have been a bathroom on the second floor just where there is one now, but the water for that deadly Saturday night bath would have been carried from the kitchen. The framing of the windows is all original and the layout of the bedrooms is probably nearly the same, though I suspect the rooms then were smaller and these have had a wall or two taken out.

But all of us are thinking about the attic. Will there be anything left there to suggest the Underground Railroad? I go up the narrow stairs and find myself in a musty unfinished space. The roof is steeply pitched and the beams, darkened with time are exposed. One is charred, reminding me of some singed letters of Nettie's. Then, right in front of me, is what we've been hoping for: a little treasure box of a room in the vast unfinished space of the attic, wallpapered on the outside like a wrapped gift, with brownish pink patterned paper from the 1850s. It is empty of furniture but bright with the sun. The interior has an old, but not original, yellow-print wallpaper. An east-facing window looks out to the back of the house where the barn would have been. At the left side of the exterior of the room is a curious tiny unfinished wooden cupboard just large enough for a man to stand in. It has a metal box lock with a large old-fashioned kind of key still inside it. An emergency hiding place, perhaps, where a slave might have been hidden and the key "misplaced." The treasure box room must have been "Bill's room," the place that the children read the bible to him or another like him. I think how hot it must have been in this stifling space on July 10, 1859, how Bill would have looked out at Nettie on her pony and heard the train whistling, awaiting his time to be on it.

★ ★ ★

When Linc's second letter from North Carolina falls through the mail slot, the one with the permission forms for a visit, I realize that the sight of these plain white envelopes with their scratchy jagged writing and their shocking return address (prisoner number 12xxxx, Central Prison, Raleigh, NC) unwraps my heart like ribbons falling from a gift. Something visceral has happened. I had not known this man since he was a small, imaginative boy. Now, like a DNA double helix, we are bound together in this curious intimate circle of correspondence. A counterpoint between the two of us, and Erastus and his children, echoing through two centuries.

Linc's story will continue to unfold, but I hope not on the front pages of the *Boston Herald*. He is on medication with heavy-duty side effects that must be harder to tolerate now that he is out of isolation and in the general prison population. The letter is full of plans, full of hope. He imagines spending long summers in Maine, working at the boatyard. I feel a pang of sadness to think of all the changes that will baffle him when he finally comes back into the world. A generation that wasn't even born will have grown up and taken charge of his summer idyll. His letter ends: I'll look forward to reading your next letter and please send one from Erastus Hopkins." I wonder if Linc really connects to these letters of Erastus, or is he just saying that to please me.

Peter informs me that next September, we are going on a trip to Stratford, Ontario, to see Richard III at the Shakespeare festival. I'm hesitant at first; I am doing my first exhibition of paintings during Open Studios in September and it will take some organizing.

I look at a map and see that Chatham, Ontario is just a little way down the road from Stratford and my mind begins to race. Bill left Erastus on July 11, 1859. He probably arrived in Chatham sometime in the month after that, maybe even a few days later. I quickly locate three historical sites and archives in the Chatham area that focus on the fugitive slave settlements of that period. It takes me only two calls to find a young African American researcher with an unquenchable passion for this history. I read her Erastus's letter about Bill. She's very quiet, but I can feel the electricity.

"Would you send me that letter? It's got a lot of information in it, and I think maybe I can find a trail and figure out who he likely was."

I tell Peter about this new idea over the breakfast table and he adds his own bit of local historical knowledge:

"Ferguson Jenkins was born in Chatham. The great baseball pitcher. Maybe we can take in a game in Detroit if we go to Chatham."

"Maybe he's one of Bill's descendents, you never know." I am thinking how graceful is the warp and weft of good marriage, woven from these threads of intersecting interests. "Wouldn't it be astonishing to be able to track some of them down? What a story that would make."

Peter looks over the newspaper at me and says, "Well it would be if one of them turned out to be Ferguson Jenkins".

We go to Chatham, Ontario and to a smaller community nearby, Buxton. Chatham today has lost its historical charm, but in neighboring Buxton, the community is much like it might have been in the 1850s, with small, well-kept cottages and white picket fences (once a rule of the town). A one-room school house from the 1840s still stands as a museum in the center of the town. The young African-American woman who gives us our tour attended it. The small number of families who live here are almost all descended from fugitive slaves. But I cannot trace Bill's arrival and it makes me sad that I cannot bring this historical connection to his third great grandchild. Despite the enthusiastic efforts of our researcher, it is impossible to know with any certainty who Bill might have been, or who living now in this community, might be his descendant. But it doesn't really matter. They are here. And we are connected.

The Black Historical Society of Chatham-Kent quotes a Dr. Disney, writing in 1857:

> "Chatham was not a mecca only. In a broader and truer sense, it was the colored man's Paris. Even now, after the experience and growth of 20 years of liberty we scarcely know a city blessed with a society more varied and refined, more opulent and gay, than was this little Canadian city during the decade that opened up the second half of our century."

Linc and I continue to correspond. He is in his eleventh year in prison.

Erastus's house on King Street was demolished in 2012. Hannah and I drove by the site not too long ago and you could see the footprint clearly in the weedy lot, with spray-painted markings indicating where the parking spaces will be. In the end, no one could come up with a viable plan for the building.

My brother Jon died in the same year. He read this book and gave me his comments before he died. He said it reminded him of his favorite poem by William Carlos Williams:

so much depends

upon

a red wheel

barrow

glazed with rain

water

beside the white

chickens

"That seems to weave together my own spirituality," he wrote, "connections, contrast, simultaneity of the particular and the general, and acceptance." He always was a person of many fewer words than I.

In the months following his death, I am in the shadow of sleep. Erastus's phrase hums through me like a warm vibration: "put your little heart in his outstretched palm and let him lead you like a lamb to do his will." I hear Erastus bidding me to surrender, and I do—to the calm of advancing time, in the Buddhist sense, the end of clinging. I practice what I learned from him: to be present, to cultivate and express my love, to soften and open my heart.

So here I am, the last of my original nuclear family, but the living head of a new branch in full bloom. I am cocooned by the living and the dead, ancestors, and children who will become ancestors.

Acknowledgments

I am very grateful to all who have helped me on this project, most especially to Sally Brady who led the writers workshop that encouraged me and critiqued the manuscript along the way. As the agent for *Erastus*, she was a true believer in the manuscript and helped me find it a good home. My fellow writers Cindy Linkas, Patty Hanlon, Miriam Weinstein, Laura Wainwright, Don McNeill, Gillian Gill, Stephanie Monahan and others gave invaluable advice at important moments. Thank you Megan Marshall for guiding me to Sally when I described the project originally.

I salute all of the tireless archivists who work to preserve the original documents from which I worked. Among these legions I thank especially Peter Drummey, Anna Clutterbuck-Cook and Andrea Cronin at the Massachusetts Historical Society and their staff who helped me with the Benjamin Kendall Emerson papers. At the Duke University Archives Janie Morris was my excellent guide to the William Swinton Bennett Hopkins papers. I am particularly appreciative of the work of Marie Panik at Historic Northampton who was my interpreter for the Hopkins archives there and who guided others with related information to me over the years. At the South Carolina Historical Society Mary Jo Fairchild made my trip south very worthwhile.

Thank you to Steve Bloomfield and the Weatherhead Center at Harvard for arranging access to the extraordinary resources of Widener Library and to Barbara Burg for her help within the library.

From the North Carolina archives I traced the thread of preservation back to Norman Boas who rescued invaluable papers from a probable trip to the dump and who then, with his wife, painstakingly catalogued them all, making my work at the Duke Archives infinitely easier. He also rescued the portrait by James Harvey Young and made it possible for me to have it restored. To Julian Dzialo, the restorer, I owe a special debt of thanks for his excellent work.

Lisa Baskin provided me shelter in the most beautiful of homes and is a lovely friend to history in Northampton, and to me.

Steve Strimer has played so many important roles in relationship to this book that it is hard to know where to begin expressing my gratitude. His role as one of the most knowledgeable people in Northampton about the fugitive slave era was key in finding the definitive evidence that the Hopkins home was on the Underground Railroad and that their house was still standing in 2011. As the leading champion of the campaign to save the house he was tireless and creative. It was Steve who put me in touch with Bruce Laurie, to whom I am enormously grateful for guiding me in the fine points of the political history of this era and the Free Soil Party. Finally, as the publisher of the manuscript, Steve Strimer is expressing his belief in this material and I am grateful for his willingness to take the risk.

To my family, my friends and all those who will find themselves on the pages of this book I am grateful, in some cases in advance, for their forgiveness of anything they may feel does not quite fit into the historical record as they recall it. I hope they will also forgive my lifting of the curtain on our very private family. Linc comes to mind especially in this regard as the rules of prisons in North Carolina do not permit any reading material to be sent to a prisoner except from a commercial source such as Amazon, so he has had no opportunity for advance reading. But his parents have read it closely and I am grateful to them for their thoughtful suggestions and support. My daughters, Josephine and Hannah Burr, from whom I always learn so much, gave me wonderful comments on the manuscript, as did my husband, Peter Altman. I am ever grateful for his superb editorial eye and gentle encouragement throughout these years of research and writing.

Notes

MANUSCRIPT COLLECTIONS

MHS: Massachusetts Historical Society

DUA: Duke University Rare Book, Manuscript and Special
Collections Library

SCHS: South Carolina Historical Society

UVM: University of Vermont Special Collections

HNM: Historic Northampton Museum and Education Center

ACA: Amherst College Archives

CHAPTER 1

8: *"Dear Nettie, How de do?"* undated: MHS

8: *"I see Swinton..."* April 3, 1852: MHS

8: *"Dear Nettie..."* May 23, 1856: MHS

CHAPTER 2

10: *"My Dear Caro...,"* June 1, 1862: MHS

11: *"My Dear Annette...,"* December 14, 1862: MHS

CHAPTER 4

25: *"This day my dear, dear love...,"* June 4, 1836: SCHS

23: Samuel Hopkins: the great Newport preacher of the same name who had
decried slave trading among his congregants and was memorialized in Harriet
Beecher Stowe's *The Minister's Wooing,* was the great uncle of Samuel and
Erastus.

27: May 18, 1835 from E. Hopkins to SB Hopkins. SCHS

CHAPTER 5

29: May 4, 1838 from Ellen Wheeler to Sarah Ann Wheeler: SCHS

CHAPTER 6

36: May 14, 1836 from Lydia Hopkins to Sarah Bennett: SCHS

40: Inventory of Charlotte Freylinghuesen Allen Hopkins' jewelry by her
daughter Sarah Hopkins: HNM

42: Letter to Grandpa Allen, Nov. 18 1866: HNM

CHAPTER 7

45: Letter from Erastus Hopkins to William S.B. Hopkins, January 20, 1860:
DUA

46: *"My Dear Father...,"* April 8 1848: HNM

52: *My Wars are Laid Away in Books, The Life of Emily Dickinson,* by Alfred Habeg-
ger, Random House, 2001, page 168.

53: Emily Dickinson Papers: ACA

CHAPTER 8

57: *The Sixteenth Annual Report of the American Society for Colonizing the free people of colour of the United States.* 1833 by Erastus Hopkins, from the Bibilical and Theological Review Vol. 5, No.2, 1833.

58: *"Dear Nettie...,"* February 1, 1854: MHS

62: *Emancipator and Republican,* February 14, 1850, Speech of Erastus Hopkins at Faneuil Hall, February 27, 1850, Phonographic Report by Dr. Stone.

62: *Jefferson Democrat,* October 23, 1856, Vol. 1. Issue 1, Monroe, Wisconsin.

CHAPTER 9

66: S. E. Bridgeman, *New England Magazine,* January 1900, pg 590.

67: H. S. Gere, *Reminiscences of Old Northampton,* 1904, pg 59.

68: Library of Congress, Papers of Salmon P. Chase, Reel 13

70: Speeches of Mr. Hopkins of Northampton on the Bill to incorporate the College of the Holy Cross, in the city of Worcester; Delivered in the Massachusetts House of Representatives, April 24 and 25, 1849. Published by Butler and Bridgman, Northampton, MA 1849, pg. 16.

74: *"My Dear Darling Daughter...,"* October 15, 1865: MHS

76: *"My Dear Sadie...,"* July 27, 1867, MHS

CHAPTER 10

79: *"gay little Louane...,* Mary Annette Hopkins to Lammie, November 15, 1861: MHS.

80: *"My Dear Darling Goslin...,"* December 29, 1861: MHS.

82: *"...And now Pussy,"* January 12, 1862: MHS.

82. *"My Dear Caro,...* December 29, 1861: MHS.

84. *The History of Lawrence Academy 1792-1992,* Douglas Allen Frank, Lawrence Academy.

84: *"Do you not remember..."* April 22, 1865: MHS.

85: *"My Dear Nettie,..."* July 6, 1863: MHS.

87: *"Dear Unknown Friend,..."* July 3, 1963: MHS.

90: *"My Dear Nephew,..."* July 11, 1859.

CHAPTER 11

93: *"Here I am...,"* June 1, 1863: MHS

98: *"The sky is overcast...,"* Feb 9, 1862: MHS

CHAPTER 12

108. *"My Dear Little Chicks...,"* February 9, 1862: MHS

110: "God's will is a profound and holy mystery...", *No Man is an Island,* by Thomas Merton, Shambhala Library, Boston, 2005, page 54.

CHAPTER 13

112: *"My Dear Sadie...,"* October 5, 1869: DUA

119: "...that land without comfort," *Christ Stopped at Eboli,* Farrar, Straus and Giroux, 1947, page 3.

119: "As I went by...," Ibid., page 85-87.

CHAPTER 14

125: *"My Dear Children...,"* December 15, 1861: MHS

129. Barack Obama, June 4, 2009 speech, Cairo, Egypt, as quoted in *The New York Times.*

CHAPTER 15

134: *"My dear sweet Daughter...,"* October 9, 1866: MHS

CHAPTER 16

137: *"My dear little Nettie...,"* December 21, 1862: MHS

142: *"My very dear son...,"* February 25, 1869: DUA

CHAPTER 17

144: *"We are here...,"* July 27, 1867: DUA

145: *Adirondack Trails: High Peaks Region,* 13th Edition, pg. 100-101

147: *For God and the People: Prayers of Social Awakening,* Boston, Pilgrim Press, 1910, pg 47.

O God, we thank thee for this universe, our great home; for its vastness and its riches; and for the manifoldness of the life which teems upon it and of which we are a part. We praise thee for the arching sky and the blessed winds, for the driving clouds and the constellations on high. We praise thee for the salt sea and the running water, for the everlasting hills, for the trees and for the grass under our feet. We thank thee for our senses by which we can see the splendor of the morning, and hear the jubilant songs of love, and smell the breath of the springtime. Grant us, we pray thee, a heart wide open to all this joy and beauty, and save our souls from being so steeped in passion that we pass heedless and unseeing when even the thornbush by the wayside is aflame with the glory of God.

CHAPTER 18

151: *"The sky has not fallen yet...,"* November 13 1866, EH to MAH: HNM

CHAPTER 21

175: "Diary of Esther Edwards," pg. 2: HNM

175: Ibid, pg. 78.

CHAPTER 22

181: Boston marriage was a term introduced by Henry James in *The Bostonians,* referring to to two women living together monogamously. Whether or not it was a sexual relationship is left entirely to the imagination of outsiders.

CHAPTER 23

187: *Rebels in Paradise,* by Bruce Laurie, University of Massachusetts Press, January, 2015, Chapter Five. For the reader interested primarily in the politics of the anti-slavery movement and the development of the Republican party, *Rebels in Paradise* is an outstanding scholarly contribution to the field.

193: "The Journal of Mary Annette Hopkins," 1856 (age 8 yrs & 5 mo). In her own hand, dedicated to her Mother: In the collection of the Emerson Family Trust.

Author's Branch of the
Hopkins – Emerson Family Tree

Esther Edwards-1695-1766
m. (Rev) Samuel **Hopkins**-1693-1755

(Rev) **Samuel**-1729-1811
m1. Sarah Williams (1726-1774)-she had five children already
and they had nine more
m2. Margaret Stoddard in 1776 who raised all the children

John b. 1770 (Hadley, MA)
m. Lydia Thompson 1773 (daughter of Thomas
Thompson and Isabella White)

Sarah Ann Wait 1799-1847
m. John Wheeler, President of
the University of Vermont

Erastus, April 7, 1810
m1. Sarah Hannah Bennett
m2. Charlotte Freylinghuysen
Allen- 1810-1890

George 1812-1830

Lewis Spring-1815

Samuel 1807

Sarah Anna 1842-1930

Maria Malleville
23 August 1843-1 Sept. 1843

William Swinton Bennett
Hopkins b. 1836
m. Elizabeth Sarah Peck

William Allen 1845-1848

Sarah Bennett
1 May 1838-26 July 1838

Caroline Dwight (Caro)
1846-1864

Mary Annette 1848-1897
m. **Benjamin Kendall Emerson** b at Nashua NH 1843

Charlotte Freylinghuysen
1849-1856

John 1850-1856

Mary Annette 1848-1897
m. **Benjamin Kendall Emerson** b at Nashua NH 1843

Charlotte Freylinghuysen Emerson b. 1874
m. Albert White Hitchcock

Benjamin Kendall Emerson 1875-1962 (MD)
m. Josephine Devereux Sewall 1875-1969

Edward Hopkins Emerson b 1877
m. Charlotte Baer Navit

Annette Hopkins Emerson b 1879
m Thomas Cushing Esty

Malville Wheelock b 1887
m. William Haller

Caroline Dwight b 1891

Sewall Emerson-b 1904
m. Marjorie Van Schaik, three children—
grandfather of "Linc"

Kendall Emerson b 1907 (MD)
m. Margaret Drew

Jonathan 1944-2012

Anne Devereux Emerson b 1946